THIS IS MY WORLD

THE CREATIVE LANGUAGE OF YIN JIULONG

RIZZOLI
NEW YORK

New York · Paris · London · Milan

CONTENTS

INTRODUCTION

Smile in the Wind: The Yin Jiulong I Know

Sunday 7 July 2024

Lü Peng

I remember the first time I met him he was wearing a black coat. He arrived at my place in Wanxingyuan, Chengdu, a young designer in search of a job. That was the day we became collaborators. With time, we would become friends.

I am in complete agreement with Kenneth Clark's view of art history: a genuine artist must have an innate gift. One cannot become da Vinci without it. How are we to make sense of the possibilities for personal growth facing a young person trying to survive in the unfamiliar environment of a huge city far from home? Despite all the knowledge we acquire from books, we remain ignorant of those ever-present underlying causes that, over time, redirect our thoughts, actions, and future goals. There is no shortage of designers consumed by their own aesthetic visions and trying to make a living in the city. In the beginning, I assumed my new friend was no different. I was well aware that the designer of one company could easily become the designer of another, or perhaps even the boss of his or her own design company. This was, after all, a path often taken by countless capable designers.

Jiulong first struck me as someone intelligent and sensitive. Prone to the occasional minor fits of temper so prevalent in his profession, he once threatened to resign. Fortunately, we decided to continue our collaboration. Today, we no longer need to discuss details and instead limit our conversations to the projects we are working on, which often leads to a colorful flurry of conflicting ideas.

The environment in which Jiulong grew up influenced his use of vocabulary and language when pondering questions:

In my childhood I was wild and natural, bathed in the grace of the heavens like any other creature, unquestioning and unaware, perceiving the surroundings with a natural vitality. Though limited, this innate spontaneity became my instinct. During my youth, life presented me with apparent hardships and compelled me to ask: Why is my life this way? Is this how it is for everyone? The answer was of universal truth, yet negative.

The continuous intervention of civilization and logic comes up short against all unforeseen, incessant, perplexing, yet inescapable situations.

Of course, we could equally argue that such thinking was an effect of the times, the social and philosophical atmosphere that influenced everyone who lived through it. However, a single era can inspire different feelings and ideas in different people:

When suffering compels you to scrutinize the life around you, it also leads you to doubt the very fabric of this world, to ask questions and seek answers. The moment you truly understand the origin of suffering is perhaps the moment of awakening.

Time flies. Twenty-six years have passed since we first met in 1998, during which time Jiulong's career has grown steadily and prominently. Most importantly, his artistic achievements, aside from being a factor in his continued relevance as a designer in this new era, have also established him as a famous artist in his own right, a status many other designers crave.

Yin Jiulong's understanding of design and art differs from what one hears among the professors and smarter students in the art academies. He places feeling at the heart of his design and art, which has prevented him from succumbing to popular tastes and cliché. "I have always been fond of animals and plants. As a child, I loved watching bees and ants busy in their rhythm, running through the grass in the morning dew under the sunlight, and observing the tendrils of melon vines coil and climb steadily until they bloomed and bore fruit…" It is in such passages that we appreciate Jiulong's sensitivity and attention to detail, and how he locates the source of art and design in these moments of vital epiphany. "I particularly love the spring. Amid the flourishing of life, I see the force of vitality but also its cruelty and compassion. Those vibrant blossoms, the gentle spring breeze—these are but the praise bestowed upon the victors, in my eyes, a testament to life's arduous struggle." There is something moving about this way of looking at the world, which brings to mind the opinion I share with Kenneth Clark, that a genuine artist must have an innate gift.

Jiulong is a mature and talented designer. Despite being involved in countless design projects, his personality and sensitivity mean that his designs remain fresh, allowing for endless interpretation. In this age of widespread materialism, he reminds consumers of the need for understanding and refinement, rather than catering to the market's frenetic demands and taste for the bright and intense. More importantly, Jiulong views design as social transformation, a means of reshaping the frameworks that govern people's thinking. Everyone knows that a single image is but a ripple on the vast ocean of society, but just as Jiulong is able to explore vast spiritual questions in the tiniest of worlds, we see in his work the possibility for design to exert a socially transformative effect.

The works of numerous photographers offer us a view of cities and villages all over China in the 1980s: defiled nature, dilapidated buildings, dirty streets, and lifeless cities. After economic reforms began in 1978, China saw a reshaping of society during which people's actions became a symbol of social reconstruction. The designer's task was no longer to approach problems guided by notions of "beauty," "modernity," or even "harmony." Jiulong makes no efforts to refashion the external appearance of the world and has no interest in concealing its old look within new packaging. On the contrary, in his search for the transformative, he turns within. Unlike other designers and artists, he does not attempt to provide so-called "aesthetic" solutions, choosing instead to find answers in the depths of the self. His moments of epiphany are born from introspection. When discussing *B.SIDE*, he said, "It feels more like a self-observation, a self-examination. Although it incorporates trendy cultural elements, it still conveys a sense of indifference and melancholy—its personality stems from that. These are all ways of viewing, though they may not seem that important. What is interesting is the emotions drawn out by the act of viewing and the place they are rooted in. This is the value I focus on in my creative process."

In the continuous flow of time, Jiulong's incorporation of art into his "design" comes across as very natural. He turns to a variety of materials to present his feelings, such as his effortless use of ceramics to convey information and narratives about life. This is also the reason his ceramic works eventually featured so prominently at Chengdu's Museum of Contemporary Art: the seamless, natural effortlessness of his creations conjure an image of the artist's flowing hair and smiling face in the wind (this is, at least, the impression the exhibition left on me). Afterward, I came to understand that Jiulong had combined design and art into a kind of inner feeling, the contours of a spiritual world. One day we met in Amsterdam when Jiulong was working on a series of ceramic pieces in the Netherlands. He departed after several days of work, leaving his creations behind, but from the photographs he brought back, I felt a deep sense of joy and delight. It would not be quite right to describe these pieces as strange, but I do believe I saw in them something of Jiulong's inner world, what I might call his "natural feeling."

Jiulong's pieces inspire people with their abundance of emotion and joy of form, but I know that they also contain the kind of solitude experienced only by artists in their quietest moments in the dead of night. Jiulong explains:

Loneliness is eternal. No one can ever truly enter another's inner world, not even those dearest to us—this, I have long understood. It indeed means that everyone lives in loneliness, but if you pay attention to the self, the Other will manifest in it. Take *B.SIDE* as an example. Its imagery undoubtedly bears trendy characteristics; this is a deliberate choice to capture the social dynamics. However, *B.SIDE* is emotionally lonely, frustrated, resolute, and endlessly unfounding.

There was a long period of time when I rarely met up with Jiulong. However, although we did not see each other regularly, I always knew that he was in the process of feeling, living, working, and thinking. I knew he was still meditating in action, lonely at work, sad when departing, happy upon returning. Jiulong does not see design, let alone art, in terms of individual projects or creations, but rather considers his life and work as a singular whole. Design and art have become his life's mission. He does not want the fruits of his labor to be mere beads scattered in space and time. He hopes, yearns even, for nothing to extinguish the light of his work, that it might forever preserve some of its radiance.

In each of my projects, I leave room for growth. I want to present each and every one of those growing, fleeting, glowing moments until they glow no longer. Many people see *B.SIDE* merely as a trendy style, and even if that's the case, it doesn't stop its form and story from continuing. If the day comes when I feel the continuation of *B.SIDE* has no further meaning to offer, I'll stop shaping it. The spaces left for expansion are meant for growth. They exist because the process of thinking, revising, and constructing continually sparks new moments of brilliance and value. When they cease to spark, it's time to stop.

This is a living account of the self, a testimony to the knowledge acquired through introspective epiphany. In truth, Jiulong is less concerned with transforming other people's souls than he is with using his art to better know himself, transform himself, open himself up, sacrifice himself. This is not simply where artistic work begins; it is the aforementioned innate gift peculiar to the artist. I have spent time working with Jiulong. We have gone on the road together, attended meetings together, and traveled together. Were it not for certain concrete needs, we would have no need to communicate. In the few decades I have been researching and writing about art history, no new art historical method or influential theoretical analysis has clouded my vision or led me to doubt what contemplation about art and personal experience have taught me about the importance of the artist's gift. What I'm trying to say is, Jiulong has this gift. It is what causes his work to be so rich in creativity and possess such substantial artistic value.

When I do meet Jiulong, what inevitably leaves the deepest impression on me is his flowing hair as he walks toward me smiling. We embrace, chat, discuss work, and, in the end, go home to work on our own projects. After he's gone, I can always see his image clearly in my mind: his smile in the wind.

1 DESIGN

Yin Jiulong has been working as a designer for twenty-eight years now, entering the profession in 1996. From 1996 to 2012, his primary focus was graphic design, and this phase in his career still plays an important role in his work today. An astute creator with a sense of social responsibility, he has always aspired to improve people's living conditions through design. His work continues to be informed by his persistent observation of, and participation in, sociopolitical change, elemental construction, and the forms, behaviors, and habits of everyday life.

Design for Yin Jiulong is more than simply an interpretation of a product. Each of his designs is a visual experiment, a creative act within a specific temporal context. He strives to situate design in a limitless space. For him, design is transformation and creation; its potential to reform society and the self takes precedence over the requirements of realism.

Yin Jiulong believes that design ought to investigate and effectively convey the context concealed behind it. Fully aware that learning and innovation depend on their environment, he ingeniously and effortlessly avoids the pitfalls of mundanity and repetition while successfully locating vital relations spanning regional traditions and artistic and cultural fields. All of this gradually comes together to form his design style: a simple, stripped-back approach, as arresting as it is restrained, that always leaves room for further exploration.

INSTITUTIONS OF CHINART

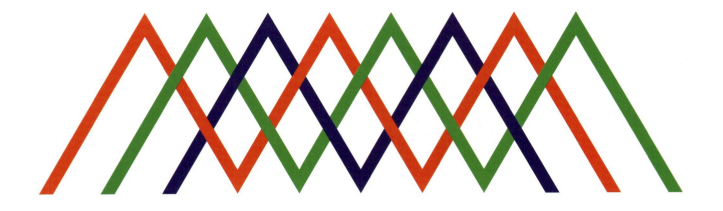

INSTITUTIONS OF CHINART

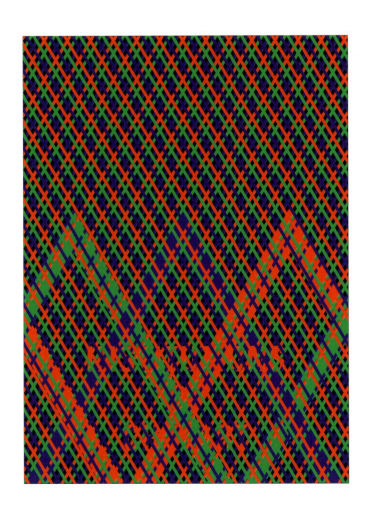

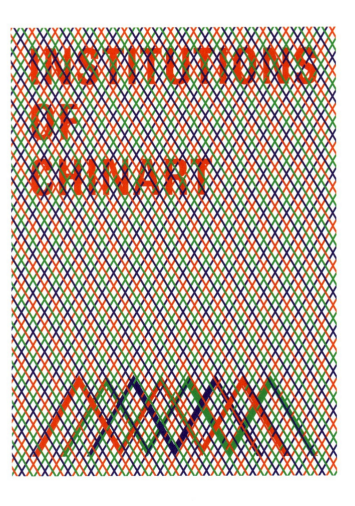

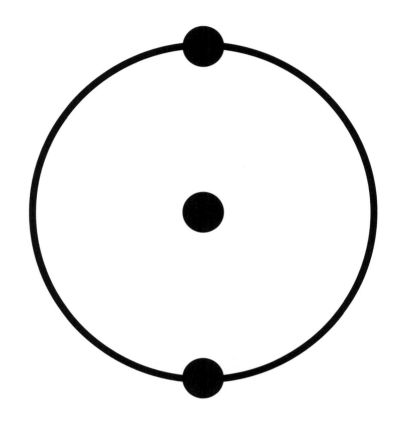

PUZHAO
TEMPLE

21

chinart valley

青城山谷

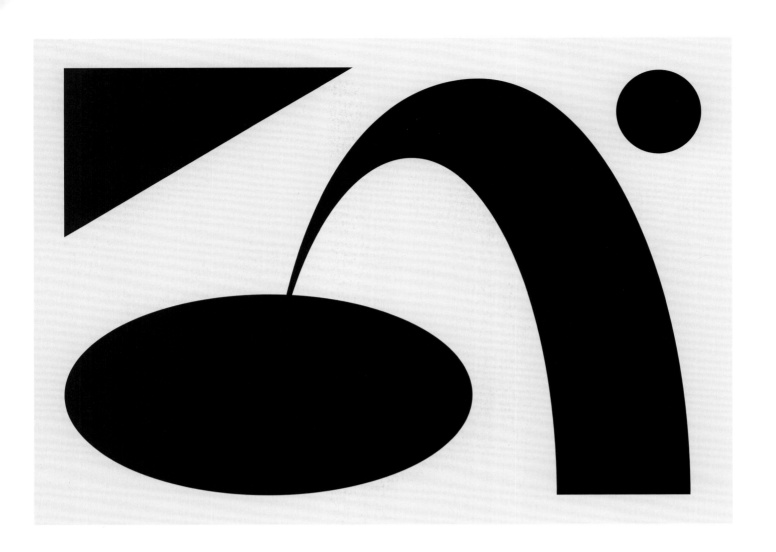

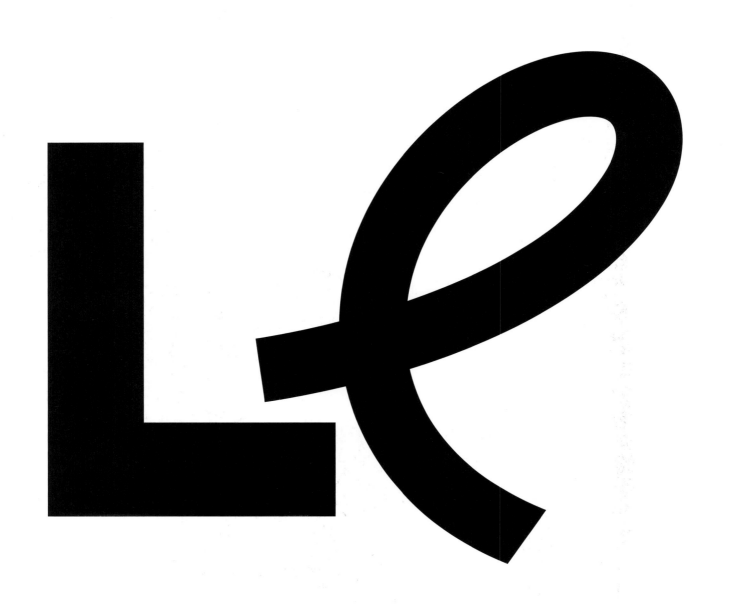

CPDf

The World Bank Group
世界银行

International Finance Corporation
国 际 金 融 公 司

CLOUdLESS

小香

酱歌

小香酱

歌

一颗大

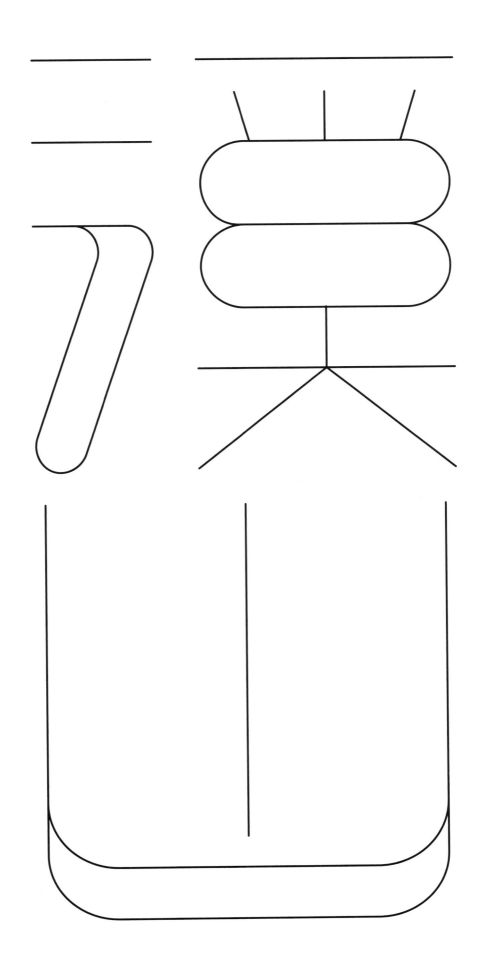

OPEN
PAGE

大视野

A

ARTLAVIE
porcelain

L

2012

V

皮小虎 ®

成都报道

maccura

美术的故事

M
Chengdu
MOCA

张大小姐

日复一日

PASSING
TIME

DURIAN
DESIGN
STUDIO

BLUEROOF

PASSING TIME

地址：广州市二沙岛烟雨路38号广东美术馆
开馆时间：上午9:00时至下午5:00时（逢星期一闭馆、节日期间照常开放）
电话(Tel)：(020)87351468 传真(Fax)：(020)87353773
ADDRESS：Guangdong Museum of Art,Er-sha Island,Guangzhou,China.
OPEN HOURS：Daily9:00am-5:00pm(Monday closed) http://www.gdmoa.org
鸣谢：广州市恒远彩印有限公司
设计：殷九龙 DESIGN: Yin jiulong

毛同强图片作品展

日复一日

展期：2004年6月15日至7月14日 展厅：第6、8号展厅
主办：广东省美术家协会 广东美术馆 江门市文联 江门市美术家协会 江门市新会区文联
协办：江门市政协书画院

广东美术馆
GUANGDONG MUSEUM OF ART

COLLECT HISTORY
CHINA NEW ART
典藏历史
中国新艺术

OPEN EXHIBITION OF CHENGDU MOCA
成都当代美术馆开馆展

CURATOR : LU PENG
策展人：吕澎

展览时间：2011年7月1日 – 2011年8月31日
开幕时间：2011年7月1日 16:00

Duration: 1st July to 31st August 2011
Open Date: 16:00, 1st July, 2011

主办单位：成都当代美术馆
协办单位：成都天府软件园有限公司
展览地点：成都市高新区天府大道天府软件园C1楼 成都当代美术馆
官方网址：www.chengdumoca.org
电子邮箱：chengdumoca@hotmail.com

Organizer: Chengdu MOCA
Co-organizer: Chengdu Tianfu Software Park Co., Ltd.
Venue: Chengdu MOCA, Building C1, Tianfu Software Park,
Tianfu Avenue, high-tech zone, Chengdu
Official Website: www.chengdumoca.org
Email: chengdumoca@hotmail.com

Chengdu |M|O|C|A|

参展艺术家：

丁乙 方力钧 谷文达 何多苓 刘炜 刘小东 刘野 罗中立 毛旭辉 毛焰 尚扬 隋建国 汪建伟
王广义 向京 徐冰 杨福东 叶永青 喻红 岳敏君 展望 张培力 张晓刚 周春芽 曾梵志

Artists:

Ding Yi   Fang Lijun   Gu Wenda   He Duolin   Liu Wei   Liu Xiaodong   Liu Ye   Luo Zhongli   Mao Xuhui   Mao Yan   Shang Yang
Sui Jianguo   Wang Jianwei   Wang Guangyi   Xiang Jing   Xu Bing   Yang Fudong   Ye Yongqing   Yu Hong   Yue Minjun   Zhan Wang
Zhang Peili   Zhang Xiaogang   Zhou Chunya   Zeng Fanzhi

BORDERS

LI YONGZHENG
SOLO EXHIBITION

2021.5.15-2021.7.18

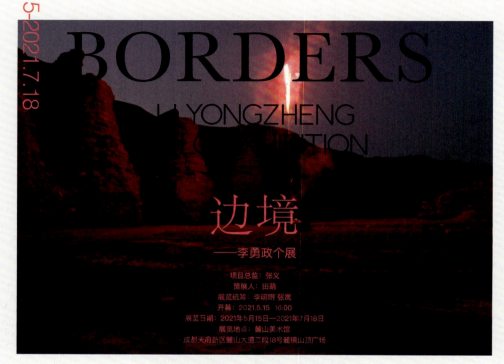

BORDERS
LI YONGZHENG
SOLO EXHIBITION

边境

——李勇政个展

项目总监：张义
策展人：田萌
展览统筹：李明明 张岚
开幕：2021.5.15 16:00
展览日期：2021年5月15日—2021年7月18日
展览地点：麓山美术馆
成都天府新区麓山大道二段18号麓镇山顶广场

LI YONGZHENG
SOLO EXHIBITION

BORDERS
——LI YONGZHENG SOLO EXHIBITION

Project Director: Zhang Yi
Curator: Tian Meng
Coordinators: Li Mingming Zhang Lan
Reception: 4:00pm SAT 15th May. 2021
Duration: 15th May. 2021-18th Jul 2021
Exhibition Venue: Luxehills Art Museum

Hilltop Square of Luxetown No.18 Section 2, Lushan Avenue,
Tianfu New Area, Chengdu, China

LUXEHILLS
ART
MUSEUM
麓山
美术馆

BORDERS
LI YONGZHENG
SOLO EXHIBITION

2021.5.15-2021.7.18

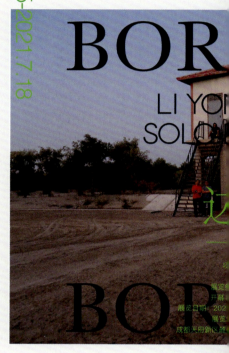

BORDERS

LI YONGZHENG
SOLO EXHIBITION

BORDERS
——LI YONGZHENG SOLO EXHIBITION

Project Director: Zhang Yi
Curator: Tian Meng
Coordinators: Li Mingming Zhang Lan
Reception: 4:00pm SAT 15th May. 2021
Duration: 15th May. 2021-18th Jul 2021
Exhibition Venue: Luxehills Art Museum

Hilltop Square of Luxetown No.18 Section 2, Lushan Avenue,
Tianfu New Area, Chengdu, China

BORDERS

ZHENG
EXHIBITION

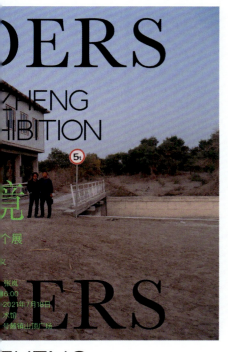

2021.5.15-2021.7.18

BORDERS
LI YONGZHENG
SOLO EXHIBITION

边境
——李勇政个展

LI YONGZHENG
SOLO EXHIBITION

BORDERS
——LI YONGZHENG SOLO EXHIBITION

Project Director: Zhang Yi

Curator: Tian Meng

Coordinators: Li Mingming, Zhang Lan

Reception: 4:00pm SAT 15th May. 2021

Duration: 15th May. 2021 - 18th Jul. 2021

Exhibition Venue: Luxehills Art Museum

Hilltop Square of Luxetown No.18 Section 2, Lushan Avenue,
Tianfu New Area, Chengdu, China.

LI YONGZHENG
SOLO EXHIBITION

Reflecting
Back
To
Countryside
文明与蛮荒
的博弈

The Game
Between The Civilized
And The Uncivilized

时间:
2023年1月31号 14:00 PM

发起人:
李国华

参与讲述者（按姓氏首字母排序）：
何　工、胡佳艺、吕　彭、李勇政、
李心沫、舒　群、田　萌、王彦鑫、
殷九龙、张小涛

发起机构:
IVA艺术、极少艺术、物质想象

主题:
每位参与者讲述一段真实的青春或者
童年时期蛮荒岁月的经历，与乡土、
小镇、小城生活相关都可以。

方式:
腾讯在线会议

2023
01.31 14:00 pm

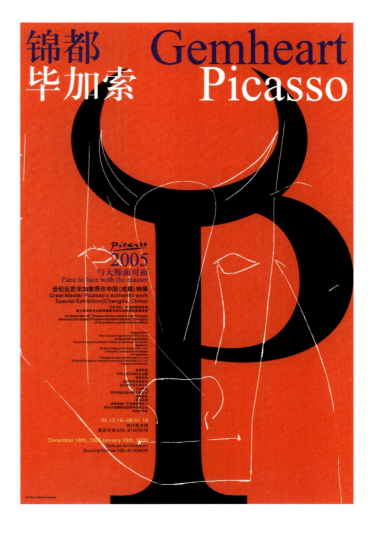

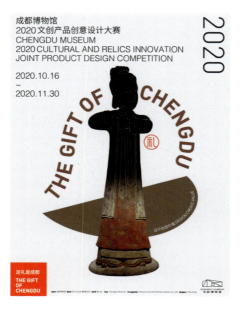

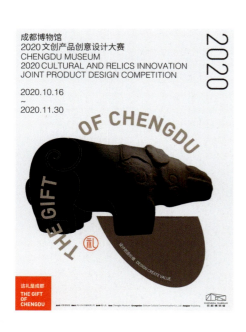

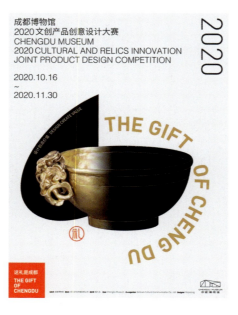

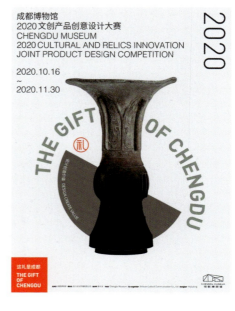

一颗大™

图片仅供参考

100%番茄汁

O蔗糖O脂肪 | NFC非浓缩还原果蔬汁

O添加人工色素 | 净含量:200mL

55

THE STORY
OF "ART"
IN CHINA

FROM LATE QING DYNASTY TO PRESENT
BY LUPENG

吕澎 著

美术的故事
从晚清到今天

北京大学出版社
PEKING UNIVERSITY PRESS

THE STORY
OF "ART"
IN CHINA

FROM LATE QING DYNASTY TO PRESENT
BY LUPENG

吕澎 著

美术的故事
从晚清到今天

北京大学出版社
PEKING UNIVERSITY PRESS

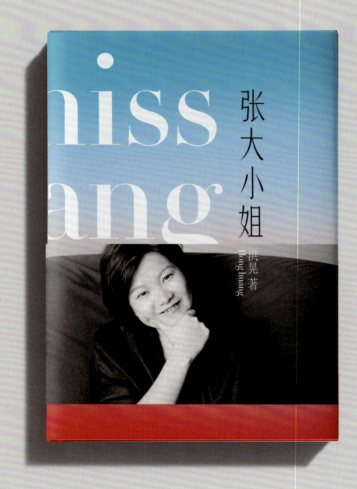

miss
ang

张大小姐

洪晃 著
Hong huang

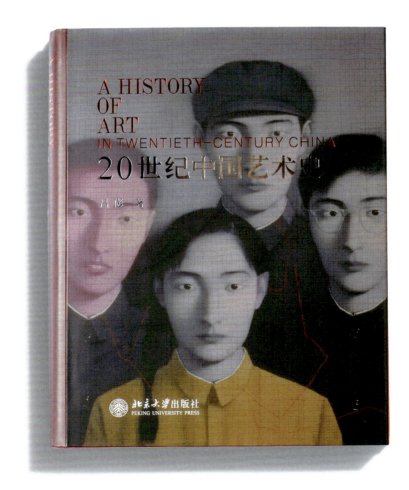

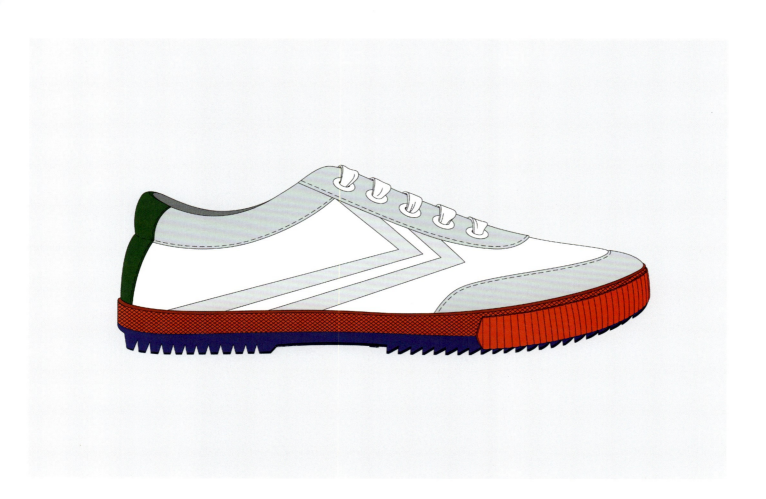

Index

Yin Jiulong's Design Solo Exhibition

About the Exhibition

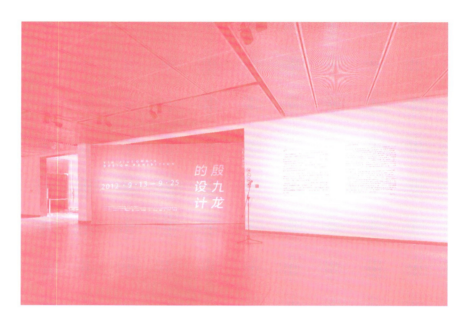

Yin Jiulong's Design Exhibition, Exhibition view, Museum of Contemporary Art Chengdu, 2012

In 2012, the Museum of Contemporary Art Chengdu held a large-scale solo exhibition of Yin Jiulong's work. Almost three hundred of his design pieces were exhibited in a space nearing three thousand square metres, presenting to audiences the story of his growth as a designer, as well as his conception of the city of Chengdu—its aesthetic, its vision, and its stylistic evolution. With his own distinct philosophy, approach to life, and artistic inclinations, he produces work that provides an insight into a whole generation of designers: the situations they encountered and the characteristics they share.

Yin Jiulong's Design Exhibition, Sneaker design work, 2012

Yin Jiulong's Design Exhibition, Exhibition view, Museum of Contemporary Art Chengdu, 2012

About the Publication

Yin Jiulong's Design, the publication accompanying the eponymous exhibition, contains the most important of Yin Jiulong's graphic designs produced in the first fifteen years of his professional career since 1996. The editorial focus of the book explores how design elements affect the creative impulse, with an emphasis on the language of design—from designing logos and typography to elemental symbols and pattern design.

Yin Jiulong's Design Exhibition, Pressed work, 2012

DESIGN Is One Exhibition

The exhibition *DESIGN Is One*: Artworks by Sun Chu and Yin Jiulong focuses on artistic creations originating from design works and ideas. In the traditional ceramics industry, the involvement of designers has always been questioned. Those who know Yin Jiulong, however, understand that his creative philosophy is inspired by his belief that design is from life, and for life. Today, Yin Jiulong's ceramic creations subvert our understanding of ceramic shapes and the aesthetics of ceramics as a living object. We prefer to refer to them as part of modern life rather than "pottery."

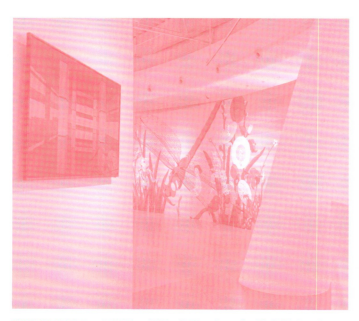

DESIGN Is One, exhibition of Yin Jiulong's works. Exhibition view at Chongqing Yuan Art Museum, 2019

DESIGN Is One, exhibition of Yin Jiulong's works. Exhibition view
at Chongqing Yuan Art Museum, 2019

DESIGN Is One, exhibition of Yin Jiulong's works.
Group photo with Chongqing Bangbangs during on-site creation

Bridge under construction in Chongqing

2 CERAMICS

Although Yin Jiulong began designing ceramics in 2010, it was the *Yin Jiulong's Design* solo exhibition in 2012 that compelled him to explore the medium in greater depth. For a sensitive practitioner like Jiulong, no design venture is "off limits." This idea particularly applies to the process of reconceptualizing his practice. Hoping to expand his understanding of the relationship between design, art, and the world, he embarked on a transcendental artistic experiment that would imbue the quotidian with art. The everyday object he settled on was ceramics. The intimate and enduring relationship between China and ceramics needs no explanation. Ceramics are integrated into the fabric of Chinese life. They are vessels that populate daily life in all contexts—from bowls and plates to cups, jugs, and teapots.

As Yin Jiulong said, "Making ceramics is a way for me to understand the world and myself. I never hoped to become a ceramic artist. Ceramics for me is simply a vessel, a medium by which to convey information about life. That is what interests me about them."

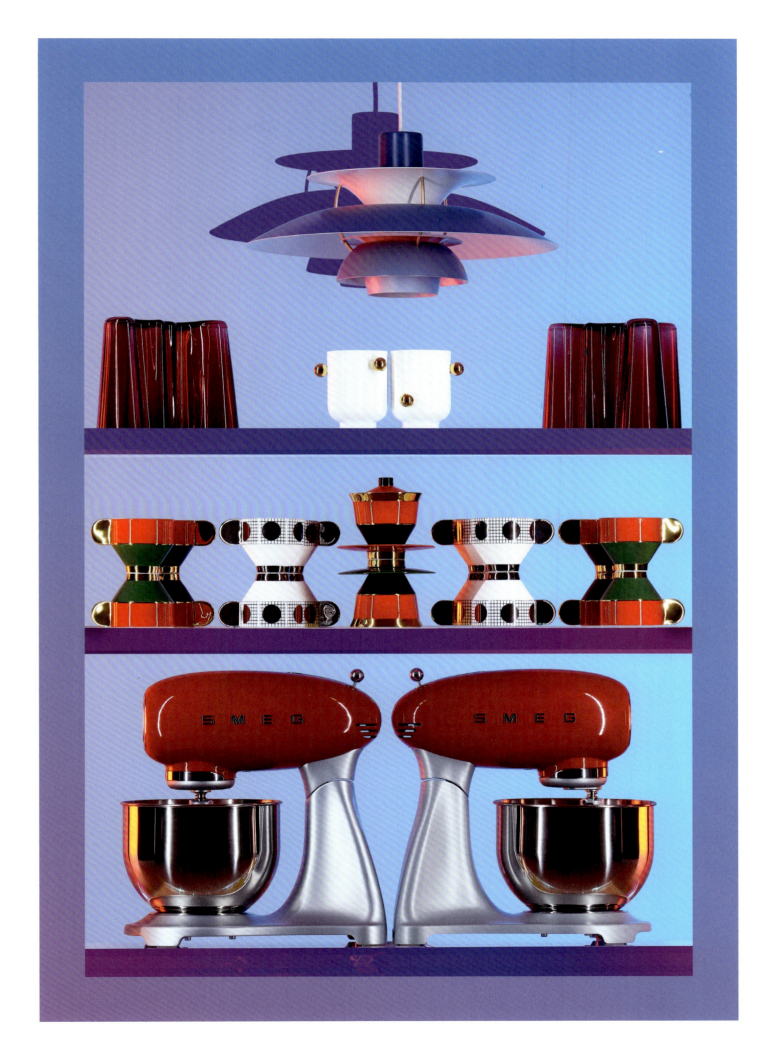

1/1000 SERIES

78

Derivatives, *1/1000* series, 2015

Derivatives, *1/1000* series, 2015

Plum Blossom cylinder, *1/1000* series, 2016

Salad bowl, mint glutinous rice and green onion, *1/1000* series, 2015

Mugs, *1/1000* series, 2015

Right Preparatory work for a magazine feature, 2015

The production process of *1/1000* series, Jingde County, 2011

Backstage

The rich history of ceramics in China spans one thousand years. The fact that Yin Jiulong's work is but a drop in the ocean of this grand tradition is the inspiration behind the name of this series of ceramic works: *1/1000*.

Struck by the sense of intimate vitality in the plum vase, Yin Jiulong endeavored to simplify and streamline this traditional Chinese ceramic vessel. He has updated the surface patterning, transforming the traditional blue-and-white motifs into visual elements more familiar to the modern eye—polka dots, rhombuses, stripes, color gradients, and solid colors—while remaining true to the traditional artisanal techniques of selecting clay, wheel throwing, final shaping, drawing, coloring, glazing, and firing.

Through the *1/1000* series, Yin Jiulong seeks to share a narrative of life in China and his understanding of its traditions. Tradition and the contemporary are not vulgar symbols or simple categories that must compromise with or exclude each other. By attempting to redesign tradition, the relationship between the past and present can be more vividly and realistically portrayed.

SONG SERIES

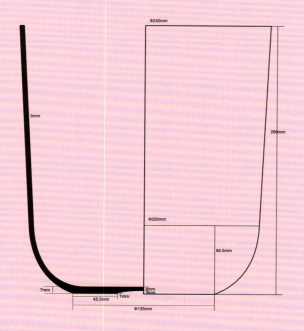

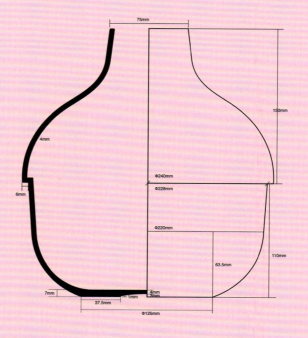

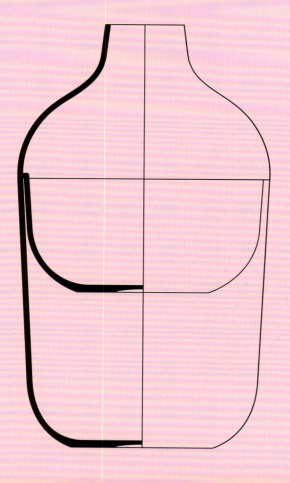

Backstage

Widely considered a period of artistic renaissance and economic revolution, the Song dynasty saw China flourish materially, culturally, and scientifically. Aside from referring to the dynasty whose aesthetic this series attempts to capture, the name *Song* also signifies a reverence and passion for the essence of beautiful objects. Remaining true to the principle of simplifying complexity, the series retains the aesthetic flavor of "Song." Yin Jiulong has always liked to observe and assess changes in people's tastes, which prompted him to split the vases in his "Song" series into two, so as to produce a range of pieces suitable for various settings and open to further interpretation. The colors tend to be simple yet striking, and the pieces can be combined and paired in various ways, making the series both practical and fun.

m² SERIES

Coffee cup, *m²* series, 2017

Tea cup with cover, *m²* series, 2019

Coffee cup from *m²* series
codesigned with the poet Wang Yin, 2017

Right Coffee cup from *m²* series
codesigned with the writer Jie Chen, 2017

Backstage

m² signifies the combination and development of two concepts, namely, the untypical mind and the creative mind.

The series incorporates the traditional Chengdu gaiwan teacup, which comes with a lid, and the classic Italian lattiera jug, which is used to froth milk for lattes and cappuccinos. Drawing from the Bauhaus style, Yin Jiulong has tightened the contours of his *m²* designs while making frequent use of clashing colors. The saucers, cups, and lids that make up the series resemble building blocks that can be freely swapped around. Some of the pleasure of these pieces lies in what might emerge from their recombinations.

A more flexible understanding of exchange is implied by the name of this series, which brings about an encounter between different cultural containers within the same field of design. The series neither emphasizes the binary between East and West nor pays much heed to the distinction between tradition and modernity. Rather, Yin Jiulong hopes to highlight how old forms can provide modern life with moments of inspiration and situational pleasure.

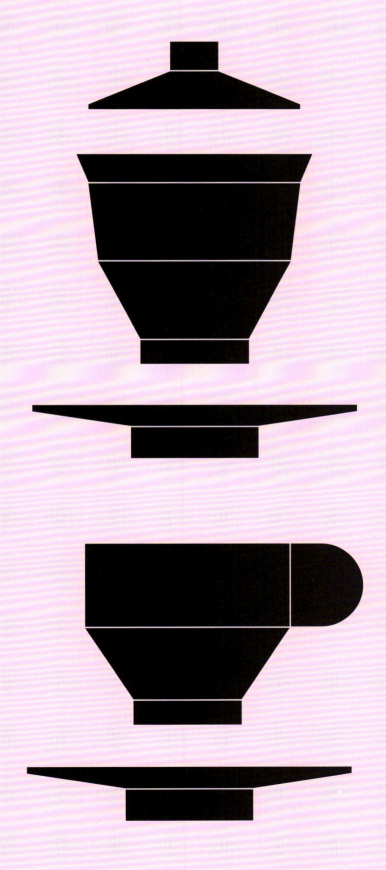

Design draft of m^2 series, 2016

WORKS FROM THE ROYAL DELFT RESIDENCY

Next page left *Hello, Delft 1*, Delft, Netherlands, 2016

Next page right *Hello, Delft 2*, Delft, Netherlands, 2016

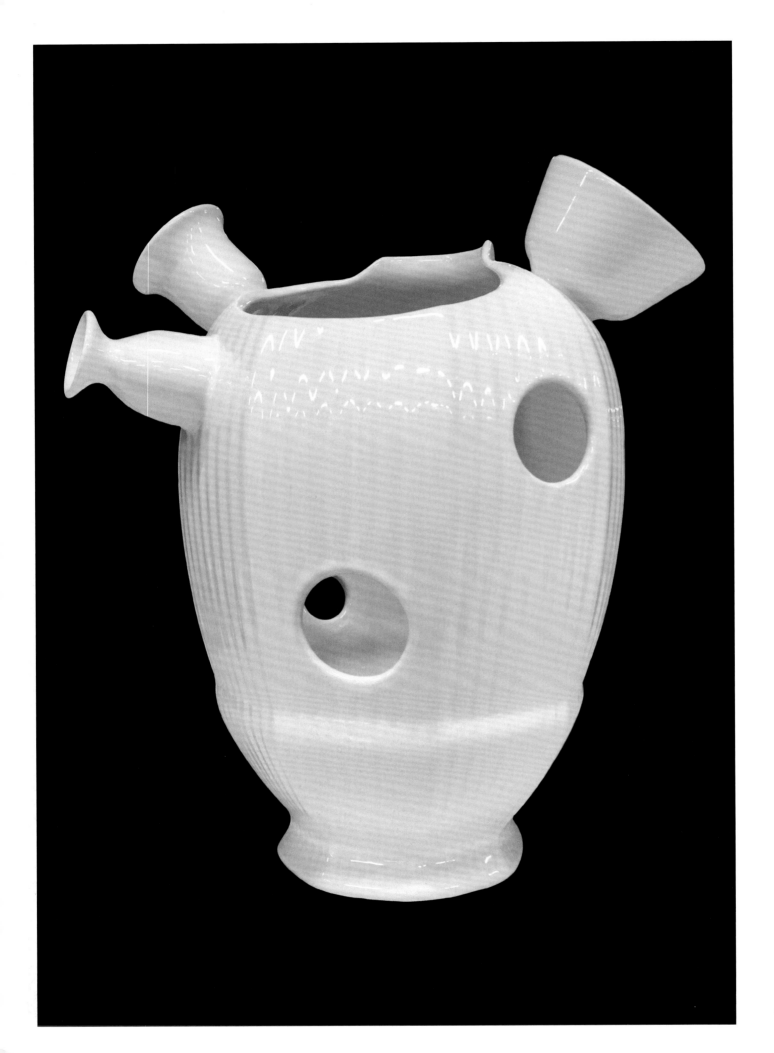

112

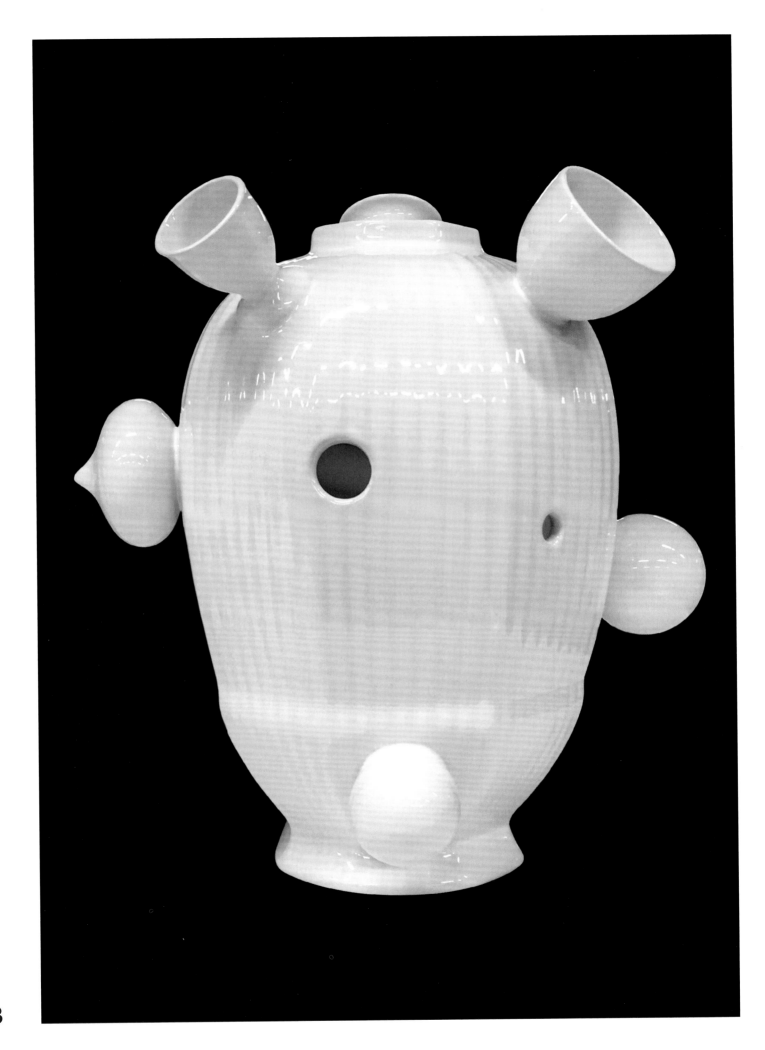

Flow, Delft, Netherlands, 2016

Coffee cup, *Hello* series, 2019

Mug, *Hello* series, 2019

The production process,
art residency project in Delft,
Netherlands

120

Backstage

Dutch artist and curator Adriaan Rees was among those campaigning for the official designation of Delft and Jingdezhen as sister cities, which increased opportunities for productive exchange between artists from the Netherlands and China. In 2016, Yin Jiulong was invited by Adriaan to participate in an official artist residency program at the Royal Delft Museum.

When Chinese ceramics were first introduced to the West, the latter's understanding of this new cultural import sometimes differed or built upon the product as it was originally conceived in the land of its origin (something that occurs in all instances of interaction across cultures). As a designer, Yin Jiulong was keen to explore the moments of resonance and divergence between such cultural conceptions. Inspired by a chain reaction triggered by numerous previous ceramic experiments, Yin Jiulong decided to make "modification" the central concept of this series. By modifying and reconfiguring ceramic forms originally produced at Delft, he created three series: *Hello, Delft*, *Flow,* and *Buddha's Long Gone*.

Apparently an expression of cordiality toward the city, *Hello, Delft* embodies a certain caution on the part of a nonspecialist making an intervention in a different ceramic tradition. In *Flow*, Yin Jiulong uses a splashing method to produce the visual effect of flowing water on the object's surface. In this series that tells a story of the Maritime Silk Road, during an era when the Dutch dominated the seas. The cobalt blue glaze symbolizes the ocean, while the white ceramic beneath seems to represent something more primordial. The story told by *Buddha's Long Gone*, on the other hand, is one about Chinese culture, which nonetheless chimes with a famous pronouncement from the West: God is dead. In the series, Yin Jiulong shares his "misunderstandings" of philosophical ideas and reflects upon life. By drawing connections between various Buddhist articles and vessels, he constructs an obscure narrative of his former beliefs and expectations.

CUP-CUP SERIES

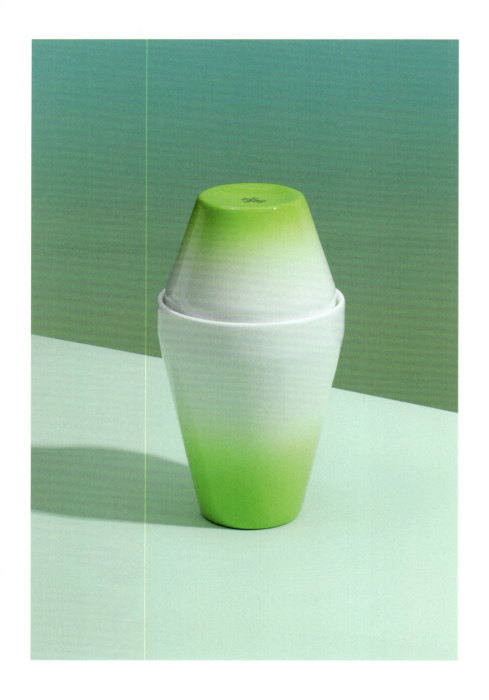

3 CULTURAL PROJECTS

For Yin Jiulong, culture is not simply heritage; it is a dynamic, ongoing dialogue that bridges past and present, tradition and innovation. Through his cultural projects, Yin Jiulong aims to both honor and transform local histories, revealing their beauty and relevance to new audiences. His work transcends aesthetics, serving as a means of fostering resilience and renewing identity among communities facing change, adversity, and the pressures of modernity.

Each of Yin Jiulong's cultural projects is an homage and a reimagining. Drawing on the symbolism and craftsmanship of regional art forms, he adapts them to resonate with contemporary life. His approach is deeply rooted in respect for the communities he engages with, reflecting their values and aspirations while creating new pathways for their stories to thrive. Through these efforts, Jiulong redefines design as a catalyst for revitalizing heritage, presenting culture not as a relic but as a vital source of connection, resilience, and shared memory.

QIANG PATTERNS AND COLOR DESIGN

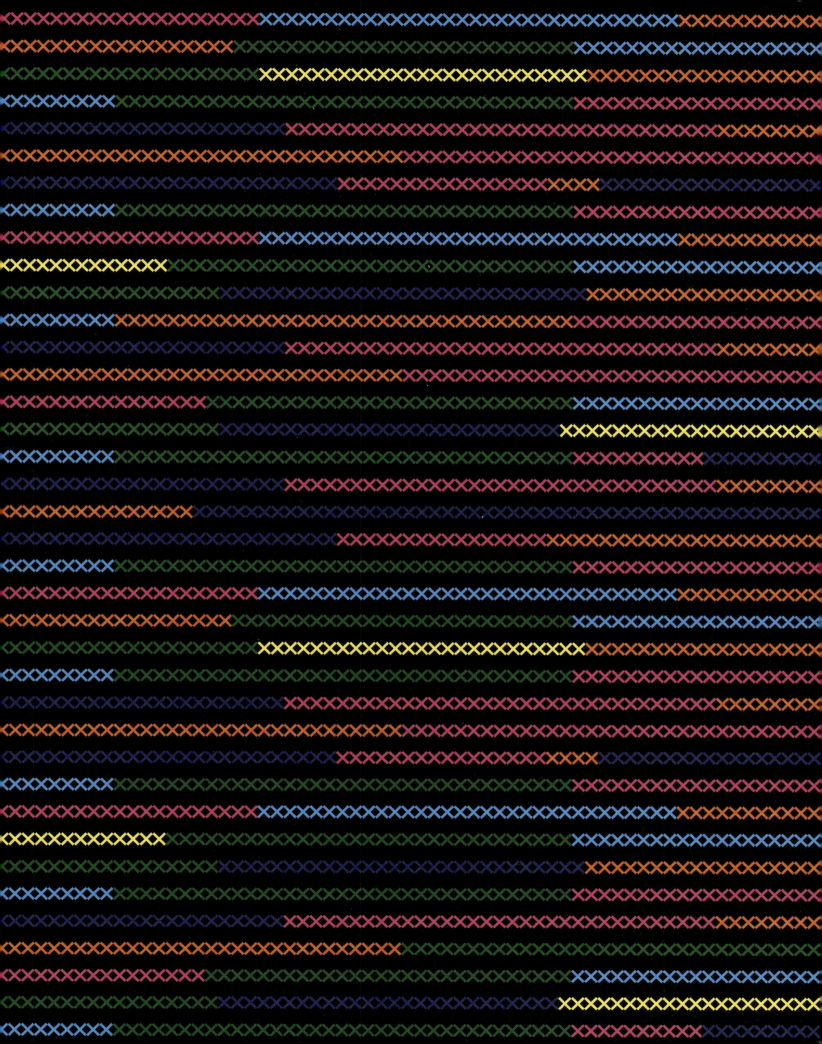

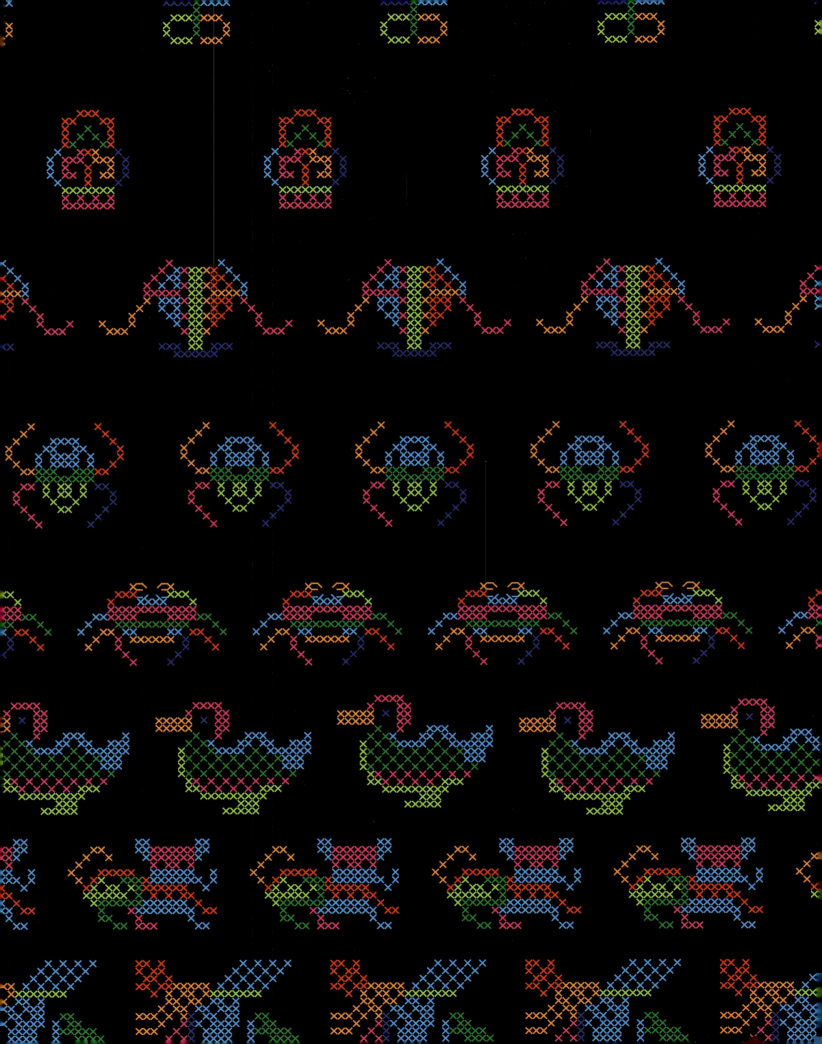

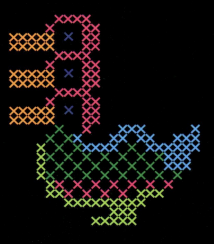

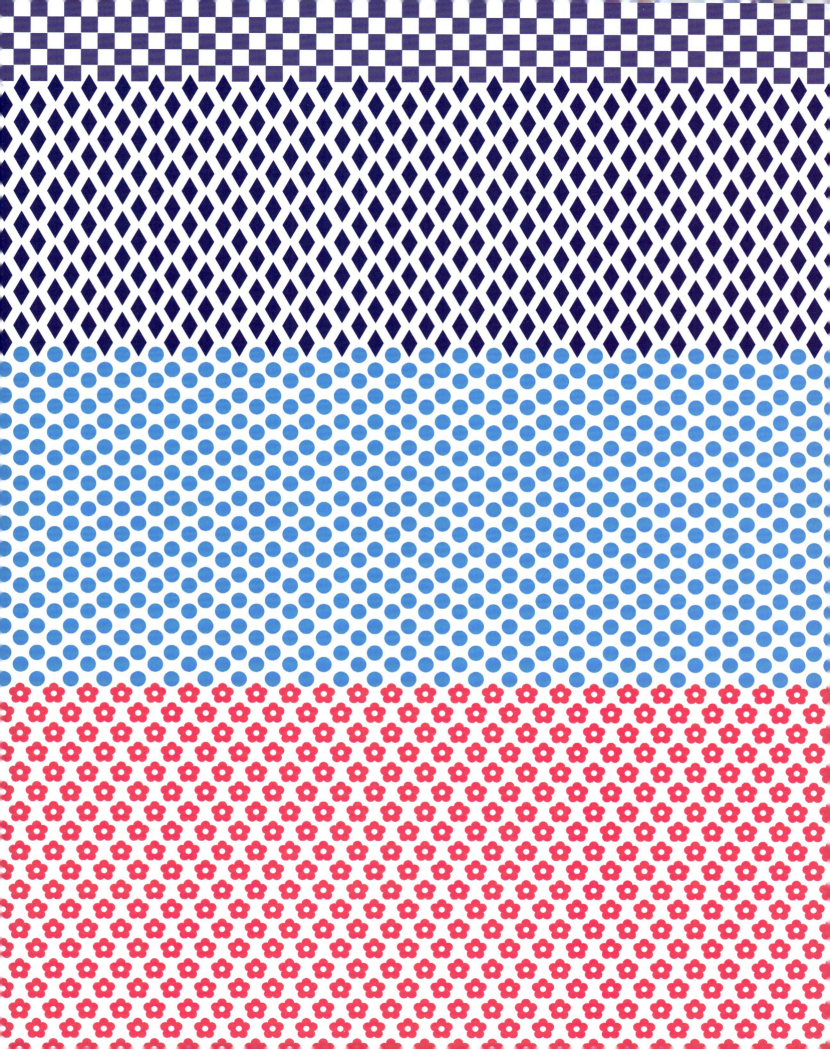

Backstage

On May 12, 2008, a massive earthquake struck Wenchuan, Sichuan, causing devastating casualties and irreversible losses, drawing global attention and sympathy. Even the typically optimistic residents of Chengdu faced severe psychological trauma. In the face of disaster, they remained resilient and supportive of one another, reflecting on the shortcomings of past social systems and honestly confronting the challenges of responding to extreme natural disasters. After the earthquake, designer Yin Jiulong participated in a relief program jointly initiated by the One Foundation and the Qiang Embroidery Support Center. This program aimed to help Qiang women from Wenchuan, who, already marginalized in their families and society, faced even greater hardships after the disaster. Yin drew from the traditional memory of Qiang embroidery, extracting colors and symbols, and hoped that through reorganization of these visual elements, the materials and product forms would align with modern aesthetics, thereby expanding their market appeal.

SHAMBHALA CAT

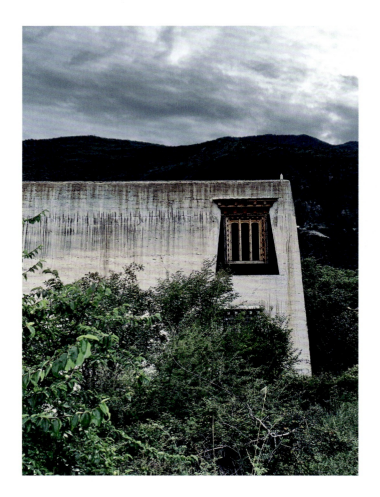

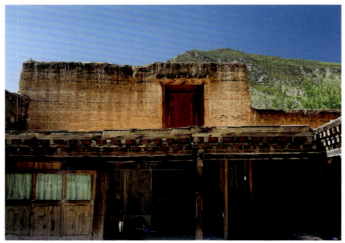

SHAMBHALA CAT IN

New Age Life.

White Tibetan house, home of Xiangcheng residents

Decorations used by Xiangcheng residents

Traditional architecture of Xiangcheng

Logo of *Shambhala Cat*

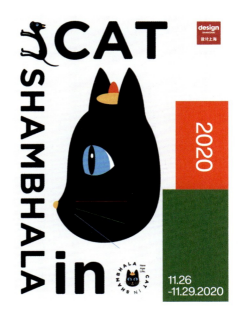

Traditional kitchen of Xiangcheng residents

Youth in Xiangcheng, wearing *Shambhala Cat* T-shirts

Shambhala Cat cultural creation poster

Shambhala Cat scarf design

Left Young Tibetan lady in Xiangcheng
wearing a *Shambhala Cat* scarf

Graffiti in the homes of Tibetan villagers that inspired the design of
Shambala Cat scarves

148

Previous and current pages Graphic design for Xiangcheng inspired by local colors, architectural elements, and natural landscapes

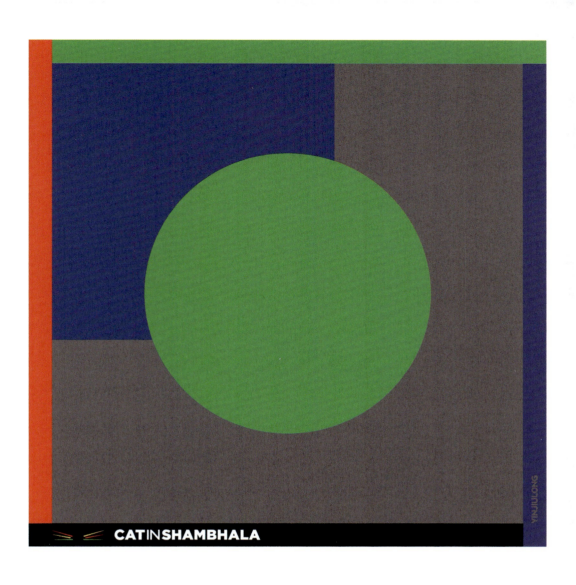

Yak wool shawl design for *Shambhala Cat,*
inspired by the decorative designs and colors of Tibetan houses

Left Buddhist halls in Tibetan family homes in Xiangcheng featuring a 400-year-old mural.

Next pages Tibetan youth in Xiangcheng modeling for *Shambhala Cat* products for advertising

Backstage

In Buddhist lore, Shambhala is a legendary, mysterious kingdom in the north of the Himalayas. For the children of these snowy lands, it is the gateway between Heaven and Earth, a place boasting some of the world's most breathtaking landscapes and contented inhabitants. According to legend, the King of Shambhala brought thousands of Buddhist teachings from India, and the people of Qagchêng, a town in the west of Sichuan Province in Garzê Tibetan Autonomous Prefecture, were said to have once journeyed to this ancient kingdom in search of the Shambhala Cat, which would protect the town from its rat infestation. Qagchêng's name comes from the Tibetan for "prayer beads in the hand," which reflects its peculiar geography of dwellings distributed in clusters along a river snaking through the valley. Sitting far lower than most Tibetan regions, a mere 2,800 meters above sea level, its altitude seems to place it where the vastness of earth meets the heavenly realm. Gazing upward, one sees the sacred snow-capped mountains; looking downward, the forests and life of the human world come into view.

The *Shambhala Cat* is the product of a regional IP project initiated by Qagchêng County. Drawing on local culture and the concept of "preserving happiness," Yin Jiulong incorporated various local traditions and myths into a cultural IP program centered on the idea of an ethnic cultural new wave. The aim of this venture is to share the story of Shambhala and preserve the traditional joys of rural life, while promoting the development of regional tourism and helping revitalize the area.

ORIENTAL
MONSTERS

Right Re-creation of mythological stories for Shadow
Puppets collection in Chengdu Museum

Visual redesign of Shadow Puppets collection
in Chengdu Museum

Oriental Monsters toy design

Oriental Monsters toy design drafts and sketches

Backstage

As a creator raised in Chengdu, Yin Jiulong has developed his own perspective and contemporary interpretation of ancient Shu culture. Drawing inspiration from the Chengdu Museum's collection and the city's most iconic cultural elements, Yin Jiulong designed a series of products combining traditional cultural elements with a modern feel. While remaining focused on cultural, practical, and emotional content, his attention to detail strengthens the connection between audiences and his designs. This approach allows his creations to transcend their original context, endowing them with greater functional, cultural, and everyday appeal. This marriage of the historical and the contemporary brings his work into a realm where art and everyday life intersect intricately and vibrantly.

If you pay attention to the self, the Other will manifest in it

A Dialogue Between
Yin Jiulong and Bao Qian (hereafter "Yin" and "Bao")

September 2023

ONE

1 Translator's Note: Blaise Pascal, *Pascal's Pensées* (New York: E. P. Dutton & Co., 1958), p. 29.

In the words of Pascal: "We sail within a vast sphere, ever drifting in uncertainty, driven from end to end. When we think to attach ourselves to any point and to fasten to it, it wavers and leaves us; and if we follow it, it eludes our grasp, slips past us, and vanishes forever. Nothing stays for us. This is our natural condition, and yet most contrary to our inclination."[1]

Existence is primarily an awakening. This dialogue begins with the quandary that rouses one man's inner journey and goes on to resonate through the decades that follow—compressed and suspended in time and space to form what appears to him as a collection of special impressions. The pains of growing up evidently left their mark on Yin Jiulong, but they also drove him to break through the universality of his surroundings. It is not that he came to understand everything, but rather that he came to realize that he understood nothing, and neither did the world around him. Such revelations are difficult to comprehend in an instant; however, life's profound paradoxes leapt up before his eyes—this truth, at least, was clear.

BAO: *One Family* resembles a story you always wanted to write. A rural extended family in a period of great historical change: typical, but also an island away from everything else. As the times race forward, it lingers in the past, and when it tries to catch up the times look elsewhere. This is the place where you were born. Is it also, in a certain sense, where your consciousness began to form. Shall we start from here?

YIN: Sure. For me, life, consciousness, predicaments, and circumstances are all primal there. I have always been puzzled by my personal growth. I grew untamed, adjusting my positions and postures while lost, caught in the relentless current of the times. I often say that only the inevitable has occurred in my birth and growth. In my childhood I was wild and natural, bathed in the grace of the heavens like any other creature, unquestioning and unaware, perceiving the surroundings with a natural vitality. Though limited, this innate spontaneity became my instinct. During my youth, life presented me with apparent hardships and compelled me to ask: Why is my life this way? Is this how it is for everyone? The answer was of universal truth, yet negative.

BAO: Confusion and awareness; a natural tendency to look back. What do you mean when you say, "Only the inevitable has occurred in my birth and growth"?

YIN: It is not just the facts that drive you forward but also your feelings. The continuous intervention of civilization and logic is no match for all of life's unforeseen, incessant, perplexing yet inescapable situations. For instance, I was born in a time overshadowed by the belief that large families bring prosperity. In my generation, there was this phenomenon of "young elders"—those who, despite their age, were treated as senior members of the family. From the moment of my birth, I found myself in the diaspora of my family, some leaving their homes, others departing from this world. People were eager to abandon old traditions and embrace the new life back then, and the roots once treasured by the family became unclear, perhaps even insignificant. Who are these people around me? What is my connection to this world? Life and awakening became the central themes of my later reflections.

BAO: What kind of awakening was it? What kind of things, moments, or exogenous forces contributed to it?

YIN: When suffering compels you to scrutinize the life around you, it also leads you to doubt the very fabric of this world, to ask questions and seek answers. The moment you truly understand the origin of suffering is perhaps the moment of awakening. When I was young, one day, a close classmate of mine was taken away from school. He wore new clothes that day, and he was so happy. I heard his family sold him. At the time it made me envious. I stood in front of the wooden window of the school and, with tears, watched his small figure disappear into the distance. In my teenage years, I toiled hard just to fill my stomach. There were moments of depleted hope, of despair-induced impulse, sitting exhausted under the scorching sun, weeping by the edge of the fields. I lose count of these experiences. Once, while speaking with Lü Peng about my life and growth, he asked me, "If you had to choose between 'arduous' and 'difficult' to describe your journey, which would it be?"
Without hesitation, I answered, "difficult." The weight of "difficulty" far exceeds that of "arduousness." It was so heavy that I had neither the time nor the energy to consider the emotional toll. Even now, I often wonder: If I hadn't fled my hometown and former life with questions in mind, what would my life be like? How should I perceive the life I know, the world I see, and the people within it? I suppose I have always been inclined first to seek empathy, to try and feel what others feel.

BAO: Indeed, you approach many situations by trying to observe and make sense of things from other people's perspectives. However, this seems a little different from what today we describe as "empathy." Rather than a kind of emotional investment, it is perhaps better described as a habitual attempt to understand the objects of your concern from their perspective, in order to better grasp their circumstances, properties, motives, and growth patterns. It is as if you are unfolding something, or perhaps validating something.

YIN: I have always been fond of animals and plants. As a child, I loved watching bees and ants busy in their rhythm, running through the grass in the morning dew under the sunlight, and observing the tendrils of melon vines coil and climb steadily until they bloomed and bore fruit—day after day, year after year. I often wondered if they ever noticed me, this giant being, growing taller and taller. Sometimes, though, I felt we were the same. Life's myriad of experiences gradually allowed me to step into the shoes of others to understand and measure the world through their eyes. However, this, too, can never truly be a state of selflessness.

You see, I particularly love the spring. Amid the flourishing of life, I see the force of vitality but also its cruelty and compassion. Those delicate blossoms, the gentle spring breeze—these elements are the praise bestowed upon the victors, but in my eyes, those are testaments to life's arduous struggle. How do others see it, I wonder? I said before that I don't want to live in the same way as the generation before me. Do you think this is a form of rejection or understanding? The many faces of life have helped me understand the differences in their ways of being. No matter how much you lament, things simply are as they are.

BAO: Understanding what it means to understand. That reminds me of some of your works and cultural projects. Understanding plays a role in *One Family*, which explores the group characteristics of the smallest collective unit during a time of historical change. Then there's *B.SIDE* and *Shambhala Cat*, both of which make their own demands on understanding, while remaining enigmatic in their meaning.

YIN: Yes, understanding what it means to understand requires certain knowledge. My family is like a fragment from a larger slice of the times—without understanding the social transformations of that era, it's difficult to grasp the nature of such family life and its underlying logic: the values they upheld, their way of living, their language patterns, and so on. Indeed, modernity, technology, and economics are reshaping the fabric of our lives, but some conditions have never changed. It's hard not to feel empathic sometimes. Take *Shambhala Cat*, for instance. When you change the logic of action through thinking, and when you incorporate the promotion of tradition and the logic of being perceived (into the contemporary perspective of life), its forms start to change. Sure, you must first understand the value of the specific regional culture, the contemporary view of life, and the pathways between them. *B·SIDE* is different. It feels more like a self-observation, a self-examination. Although it incorporates trendy cultural elements, it still conveys a sense of indifference and melancholy—its personality stems from that. These are all ways of viewing, though they may not seem that important. What is interesting is the emotions drawn out by the act of viewing and the place they are rooted in. This is the value I focus on in my creative process. If there is any validation to be found, it is in discovering and capturing those emotions while viewing.

BAO: Did any long-lasting periods of doubt or difficulty arise during this process? On the one hand you have been able, or at least willing, to develop a solid understanding of what is eternal in life. On the other, however, you have always looked to another plane of truth inhabited by those things that concern self-consciousness.

YIN: I am often certain of the sense of doubt I have toward myself. For example, am I truly sincere and authentic? Or do I align with society's broadly accepted values? Alas, I am often questioning myself.

170

I treat this self-awareness with great seriousness, but in everyday life, it often seems detached. I acknowledge its importance only to dismiss it soon after—it is merely what it is. Whether I hold on to or disregard it, this self-awareness always leaves me in the pull of detachment and implications of the everyday. As for existence, I focus on the reality I see, but I also care about my spirit's meandering. I see the tendencies of awareness as part of the very existence of life itself. Finding myself in these unchangeable circumstances of our time and the specific conditions of living in this very moment, I stay vigilant—and in that vigilance, I find moments of contentment. I believe, without a doubt, that there is something beyond life.

BAO: "There is something beyond life." By "life" do you refer more to what exists, or the experience of everyday life? Of course, both are concepts with their own systems and ambiguities.

YIN: I believe that existence is a fact. This fact is not only the phenomenas themselves but also our perception of them, and it includes imagining what lies beyond what is known. The everyday, too, is a form of life's expression. Though it may appear ordinary, it's a complex, intricate, and direct response to lives layered upon one another. I let go of the sense of seriousness in some of my works; I tend to overlook certain things while fixating on others. I try to place things into the natural flow of emotion, though I have yet to rationally think through or measure this approach. When I say, "There is something beyond life," I think I am trying to describe something that edges closer to the unknown— a realm encompassing both perception and what lies beyond it. I often wonder if there is some unseen force beyond, and if so, perhaps I am a part of it. In that case, differences and unknowns that are difficult to reconcile might achieve a kind of equality on this deeper level.

TWO

2 Translator's note: This is a quote from Zhuangzi, the Daoist philosopher of the Warring States period. For reasons of legibility, we have offered here a simpler rendering than the more scholarly rigorous translation by A. C. Graham: "It is inherent in a thing that from somewhere that's so of it." (A. C. Graham trans., *Chuang-Tzŭ*, London: Unwin Paperbacks, 1989, p. 53.)

Consciousness flickers in and out of view. He earnestly awaits moments of self-consciousness, to which he attaches great importance, but their arrival only convinces him there must be more to them than he can grasp. However, when the thinking faculties are at rest, the shapes of perception begin to stir. His tendency to anticipate people's experiences allows him to empathize with the eternal predicament of others. He firmly believes that "Inherent to a thing is that which makes it so,"[2] and as such, likes to observe the elements that constitute what people perceive and feel, especially those that enable mutual recognition. Existence itself should not be ignored. He considers his self-recognized exceptionality as belonging to another universality, one directed at psychological truth. There is something, he believes, beyond life. Through the metaphorical reality, conceptual exit points, and interrelated reconstructions that characterize his work, he marks the limits of imagination between self and Other.

BAO: Let's talk about contradiction. From your experiences growing up to thinking about things, from expressing yourself to adopting new identities, you must have faced a series of conflicts and contradictions. To really understand these difficulties is itself a difficult task.

YIN: No matter how it is understood or felt, contradiction always sparks immense conflict. These conflicts, in turn, often recall pain, as you mentioned: to really understand difficulty is itself a difficult task. At times, I feel that difficulties and conflicts are ever-present in my life; they come in unending succession, one after another. I imagine this might be the case for others too. Could this be the very nature of vitality and desire? If so, I see it in two forms: the problem itself and a free-flowing source of imagination. The former, I believe, requires no excessive worry. The latter, I might perceive as either a problem or a spark, much like how we view desire and need. I have gained much validation in dealing with these contradictions and conflicts. I wonder, though: does this validation come from the understanding of the result, or from a shared empathy with the process? Of course, either way, it is not anything extraordinary.

BAO: In the animal figures that appear in *B.SIDE*, we see these almost complete arcs. Actually, something similar appears in an earlier piece, *Portrait of Spring*, with its downward curling paths. Perhaps there are even earlier examples. In your more recent *The Plan of Everything*, the arc seems to suggest a space between imagination and the real. On an intuitive level, something about it rouses a certain melancholy in me. What I'm trying to say is that where there is contradiction, there is tension, and tension can appear in many forms, for example in solitude and as part of a collectiveness.

YIN: Loneliness is eternal. No one can ever truly enter another's inner world, not even those dearest to us; this, I have long understood. It indeed means that everyone lives in loneliness, but if you pay attention to the self, the Other will manifest in it. Take *B.SIDE* as an example. Its imagery undoubtedly bears trendy characteristics; this is a deliberate choice to capture the social dynamics. However, *B.SIDE* is emotionally lonely, frustrated, resolute, and endlessly unfounding. Well, *The Plan of Everything* speaks of life forms in a manner closer to animism, where objects are understood from the perspective of their natural life attributes. The way I see it, when objects are perceived and imbued with emotions, life leaps out before us. This awareness of life often colors the world with its melancholy of seasons passed, and even though this kind of perception is limited, it really happens. These tendencies toward emptiness, growth, grandeur, and dissolution—aren't they us? Even without considering the individual differences in perception, why does a collective often present a more comprehensible appearance? Is it that they are somehow less intelligent than individuals? This kind of thinking is clearly unfruitful. The collective often displays a kind of tendency, one with more defined and recurring choices that reveal the soil in which it grows, the paths and logic that guide it, and even its restrictions and attempts to break free. I incorporate this appearance into my psychological value system, or what I call psychological truth (otherwise, observation becomes ineffective, and empathy is impossible). Until I have formed an effective perception and understanding of the underlying logic, I am reluctant to express anything through my work too promptly. Projection is always triggered by an understanding of life. Whether from the psychological truth of the Other to mine or the reverse, it makes no difference. What matters is that, in the end,

172

we either see ourselves in the Other or we are bridging the gap between one another.

BAO: Before you begin observing something, or enter a state of creativity, do you have to face reality from a position of transcendence? Just as Wittgenstein said, "The world is all that is the case."[3]

3 Translator's note: Ludwig Wittgenstein (Ogden/Ramsey trans.), *Tractatus Logico-Philosophicus* (London: Kegan Paul, 1922), p. 403.

YIN: I like this idea. I would say there exists a kind of natural law. I enjoy identifying the inherent qualities of objects and forcibly inserting some of my own ideas into them. The object's intrinsic attributes take on symbolic meaning. When an emotionally imbued object is reintroduced, the emotions you seek to evoke can find a comprehensible trait, and their form comes to life. The way the silicone strips are presented in *The Plan of Everything* belongs to this latter category.

BAO: Your recent work has drawn specific emotion from intricate situations, like in *One Family*, and presented abstract and open interactions divorced of context, as observed in *The Plan of Everything*. Whether it is a state of self without self, or the real feelings released by abstraction, these pieces outline a metaphorical reality. Do you think they could become a societal form?

YIN: Yes, on the one hand, I have always believed that everything revealed through the extension of perception and thought counts as a kind of fact for me, a part of my personal truth. In this context, my experiences and thoughts are based on the limitations of my judgments, yet perception sometimes transcends those limitations. On the other hand, if "the world is all that is the case," then I believe that sociality is a partial reality presented by the real world. This reality always manifests in a certain way—tangible and perceptible, a phenomenon that can be both concretely described and abstractly summarized.

BAO: This touches on the question of psychological truth and underlying logic. Barring occasional departures, has this been a consistent concern of your work from your early years as a designer to today?

YIN: I have always thought that the underlying logic of things reveals some fact-based information—it's just a matter of whether the observer can be keen enough to receive, capture, and understand it. Just like quantum entanglement, when the observer engages in the act of observing, the quantum particles escape. This "fact" is a natural release and understanding of information.
No matter how someone behaves, their true intent is always revealed. At least that's how it is for me. When I was young, no one asked me to do design, nor did anyone tell me how. It was just an impulse, a feeling that a design was needed. I thought I was expressing something through that design, but in reality, I was just articulating my understanding of it. It was, in fact, even imitation—not of someone else, but of a method I was then constructing. Through this method, I ultimately arrived at a state where I could see myself in the Other and the Other in myself. Even today, I look back and still see the many paths of authenticity that, though appearing to be growth somewhat tainted, still lead back to their origins. In fact, I think that was my

most authentic phase—growth built my cognition, but in the accumulation of that cognition, my original self remained unchanged. That authenticity was clear. Doesn't creation itself need to stem from an inner truth? It's not just about form. The truth I speak of now, even if buried under layers of dust—so what? Often, the truth and freedom revealed under the constraints of limitation are the most refined.

BAO: Whether it's your recent work or our current conversation, I perceive in you a powerful sensitivity to the facticity and symbolism of things and phenomena as such. Do you think this sensitivity is innate or is it something that can be attained through cultivation? And at the same time, how does one keep it in check?

YIN: My sensitivity, I guess, came out of my insecurities. In moments of fear and anxiety, I can really focus and gather information. Sometimes, this means quickly identifying the crux of an issue to speed the process of sorting and judgment—if you see it in terms of efficiency. In terms of observation, when I was in university and encountered works that interested me, I would often ask myself: under what circumstances did the artist develop such thoughts? I might not be able to judge or recreate those conditions accurately, but I found a way of reading through this process.

BAO: In *The Plan of Everything*, forms like strips (such as silicone strips, hemp rope ecc.) interact with other material forms, which include existing items with their own material properties, such as pottery or the picture frame. As such, the arrangement of silicone strips increases the tension between object and imagination while providing a broader view of emotion and the intention of life. Are you particularly concerned with the world of objects (including their constitutive elements)?

YIN: I've always noticed, both in myself and the people I interact with, that we often overlook what's around us. Even when we say "paying attention to the everyday," we aren't necessarily focused on the everyday itself but measuring its value. I was like this for a long time. Fortunately, self-reflection can feed back into behavior, so much so that I become more willing to present what I perceive in concrete terms through cognition. As a result, I've become more inclined to observe the elements that help construct what we know and feel, particularly those that help us recognize the Other. These elements build a tangible reality, perhaps even offering revelations—revelations that many need, but are often attributed to words of social action such as identification, selection, combination, transformation, and translation. Existence itself is overlooked. In *The Plan of Everything*, I chose from a wide range of materials and forms. Some materials were already there, while others were modified from their original forms. I used factory custom-made silicone strips of different shapes, lengths, thicknesses, flexibility, and densities to shape the pieces. Sometimes, making these works felt like planting seeds. It wasn't anything special, but the works seemed to take on a kind of vitality. Of course, they may also contain messages of destruction, reconstruction, or frustration. By incorporating industrially manufactured objects, I wanted to make the pieces into lives that are lifelike yet unalive.

174

BAO: Material has the property of growth, and so do relationships. When dealing with multiple conflicting relationships, you do not resolve them by avoiding or homogenizing them. You retain the particular characteristics of individual elements, sometimes even emphasizing them. In what appear to be unreconcilable relations, you might leave an opening. Is this in order to approach the possibility of a kind of balance?

YIN: For millennia, all have suffered, and why? There is a reason for it, and in its core lies human nature. As I see it, history often mirrors itself in startling ways because certain inherent qualities of human nature make it so. I rarely bring up self-reconciliation; mostly, I try to understand as I move in parallel with time. It's about acknowledging established facts and, on top of that, dissolving them.
A creator should be multifaceted unless they've found their final exit. I am full of contradictions and I am multidirectional, and this brings about my versatility. That's why I don't abandon any phases of my thought. I don't pose as a prophet—if anything, it feels as though these sources are the ones revealing things to me. In each of my projects, I leave room for growth. I want to present each and every one of those growing, fleeting, glowing moments until they glow no longer. Many people see *B·SIDE* merely as a trendy style, and even if that's the case, it doesn't stop its form and story from continuing. If the day comes when I feel the continuation of *B·SIDE* has no further meaning to offer, I'll stop shaping it. The spaces left for expansion are meant for growth. They exist because the process of thinking, revising, and constructing continually sparks new moments of brilliance and value. When they cease to spark, it's time to stop.

BAO: Do you have any relatively constant requirements underpinning your decisions to adapt and recombine the relationships between perceptual objects during artistic creation? What is it that usually causes these fluctuations?

YIN: I see this kind of stability as a habit—like the definition of a certain style or the subtle control of idiosyncrasies. I detest production mechanisms that grow out of habits. In a sense, the more familiar something is, the more frustrating it becomes because familiarity affords predictable directions and outcomes. When precision and stability reach a certain level, there's a risk that the excitement or interest gets diluted or even lost within defined and classified styles—that's how I understand it. As for today, I want to break away from past systems, though it's a challenging process (as I have to learn to embrace some spontaneous reactions). I've noticed some promising signs in my thinking and creative progress lately. My sensitivities bring in a sense of immediacy that seems closer to what I want to express. And this fluctuation actually stems from a fundamental desire—it's difficult, but it is clear and real.

175

THREE

The quality of hybrid reality, open interaction, psychological truth through mimicry...
All are interesting forms that, like faces, call for dialogue to transplant or translate
the reality that concerns him. He often remarks that his theoretical and systematic
thinking is lacking, but he consistently reaches new heights of consciousness
through personal experience and perception alone. How much change is needed to
satisfy the emotive need for change? In confronting his work, people find themselves
oscillating between states of alienation and resonance, encountering psychological
existence that seems to lie both within and beyond them. For him, art is both a
means for the soul to express itself and an inherent response to this expression, for
which only life can provide a profound, immanent, and enduring explanation.

BAO: Your recent works, including some projects that have yet to be revealed
to the public, seem to share the quality of hybrid reality. Is this
transcendental premise something from beyond, or is it an escape from
the limitations of daily experience?

YIN: In this hybrid reality, objects, symbols, and even historical contexts
that the audience is familiar with are both a prelude to empathy and
facts themselves. As for the other system based on this reality, I feel it
resembles something closer to the truth—where interests, facts, and
questions intertwine.
The trendy, fashionable language of *B.SIDE* and the strip-shaped in-
stallations in *The Plan of Everything* appear within the viewers' empirical
perception; they draw one into the artist's true creative intent.
The ultimate ends are the interests, facts, and issues constructed
through the artwork. This process mirrors the moments when we
confront ourselves—it is synchronous. Creating something out of
nothing in art is an important mode of expression. Where there is
transcendence, there are also omnipresent limitations. These are fundamental issues. The limitations I encounter—whether they are expe-
riential, structural, systemic, or grounded in reality—seem to come in
stages. For me, they often lead to a sense of finding light at the end of
the tunnel. I don't believe I can lift these limitations for others. What
I think I can do is present something with more narrative, something
understandable, enlightening, and filled with possibility. After all, only
those who resonate on the same frequency can truly connect—otherwise, this world would have already become a better place.

BAO: In the artworks and products you create, you like to leave room for open
interaction. Is there anything in particular you want to present or
understand through this interactive potential?

YIN: I really like the tall and short ceramic cups from the *1/1000* series.
These cups were redesigned by scaling down a traditional Chinese
plum vase to an appropriate size and then splitting it into two. This
was the first time I achieved a form of self-observational interaction,
which I found interesting. In my later works, I tried to understand why
most people try to change their lives, comprehend and search for the
driving force behind this desire for change, and how significant those
changes must be to satisfy their emotional needs.
It's like in our student days when we covered our dorm rooms with
posters or moved our bed to a different spot in a rented room. We were

simply looking for new feelings through change. People often crave the new and get tired of the old, except for when we experience nostalgia. In truth, as long as you honor emotional shifts, even in small ways, the space for interaction emerges.

In *The Plan of Everything*, this interaction becomes even more apparent. We deliberately left room for derivative connections—for example: What happens when this form interacts with objects in our daily lives? What if someone replaces the silicone strips with another object? Or what if natural, biomorphic forms are continuously layered on the silicone strips? These considerations bring a sense of anticipation and excitement to *The Plan of Everything*.

BAO: Some words have cropped up during our discussion: metaphorical reality, open interaction, psychological truth, underlying logic, and so on—or perhaps you have other, more precise expressions? In your recent works, how do they come together to produce meaningful forms?

YIN: Open interaction begins with the superimposition of interests. We know art is realized through viewing, but participation can transform its concepts. With their aesthetics, worldviews, and personalities, the participants constantly interact and exchange with the artist so that the artwork is no longer isolated. As for psychological truth, *The Plan of Everything* is created with a mimetic approach; the issues we discuss are often based on the intention of life itself. I hope to use the artwork's imagery and the feelings it invokes to construct some causal relationships and build a psychological truth through mimicry, to reexamine life and the meaning it imparts: the stirring of the human heart, prompted by objects. Life, consciousness, objects, emotions, openness, and interaction all foster the regeneration of the artwork's vitality.

BAO: That being said, life's increasing diversity cannot make up for people's neglect of its essence.

YIN: Yes, that's exactly what I mean. Life has always moved me deeply. On one hand, it is resilient and tenacious, almost like an interaction between physical existence and consciousness. As long as it exists, consciousness will always seek to provide a rational explanation of existence. On the other hand, it is incredibly fragile—sickness, separation, death—all irreversible, with no way to look back or reshape things (even if this might push us closer to the origin of meaning). Metaphorical reality, therefore, becomes a part of artistic creation, and this part reflects the life forms that the tides of the times impose on the individual. If there is an ideal form of life, then metaphorical reality becomes crucial, as it is through this that we begin to contemplate the essence of life itself.

BAO: You have constantly attempted to move between artistic forms and media—from graphic design and product design to cultural art projects, regional cultural IP and artistic creation—and many acknowledge what you have achieved in each of these fields. What do you think about when you are in a period of transition? For example, are there any rational or emotional factors that could be called driving forces?

177

YIN: It's really an emotional escape. I've always had a strong sense of crisis, and looking back, this crisis seems to stem from anxiety about time. In my past work and life, I always wanted to distil a form of talent from change—you see, I dabble in many things (laughs). Of course, this is also driven by the need to generate creativity in my profession. Later, and even now, this anxiety about time continues to push me toward change. I've always felt that life does not come easily, so it would be a shame not to do more.

Alongside this, in my work environment, is a sense of curiosity—curiosity drives me to seek change. Every stage of life has its necessary experiences, but the one constant is the search for new creativity in my work. When I achieve that, it lifts my spirits, and I immediately begin to look forward to the next creative idea. When I'm dissatisfied with the frequency or the outcome of my creativity, I start seeking new paths for change, like shifting from graphic design to three-dimensional work, space, products, etc. Now, I'm going through another transition, though I believe this may be my last. Because art has been the one constant I've craved throughout my professional life, I believe it is my enduring pursuit—unless, of course, I reach a point where art no longer holds any importance for me.

BAO: In the current moment, what is it that you are most sure of? What are your thoughts on it going forward?

YIN: Today, the only thing I'm sure of is how to continue living freely, which for me probably means creating. Why use the word "living" and not just "creating"? Because if living and creating alternate in this way, their roots will reveal themselves. Everything will naturally present itself, and any changes in the status quo will require courage. I don't have many thoughts about the future—perhaps it's just a purification of my understanding of life, like living and creating more quietly. In today's world, even that feels like a luxury.

BAO: How do you regard the identity of a creator? Through the act of creation, what do you most want to break through? What do you most want to balance?

YIN: I used to be deeply conflicted about my identity as a creator, but now I prefer to approach the true motives and sincerity of my work with ease and openness—why do I create? In creation, what I want to break through the most is my observation method, which is the inspiration and presentation of ideas. Over time, I hope to explore more natural modes of expression. I want to reach an equilibrium between my work and the time we live in—whether I can form a deeper connection to our time and how I can immerse myself in it and manifest myself. This may align with what I call natural logic, which resembles the organic growth and development of things and life.

BAO: Do you feel possibility takes precedence over reality? Of course, we can limit the scope of this question, perhaps to how it concerns your future self?

YIN: For me, the possibilities always take precedence over reality. Although the limitations imposed by the objective realities of the world are not easily escaped, from my experiences, challenges, and the results I've achieved, this is how it seems.

BAO: Briefly, how would you describe what artistic creation means to the past and future you, whether in terms of the excitement you feel, the difficulties you face, or the support you require?

YIN: To me, artistic creations alter the face of the past, and for the future, they signify a true interaction with life, which I find more meaningful. From a linear perspective of time, many might think it's too late, but for me, it's just right—that's the inevitability of reality. The shifting conditions of creation and new modes of expression excite me greatly, and when I think about the future, I believe the best time will be about five years from now. As a creator, I've gained a lot from creating. I'm not sure what kind of support an artist truly needs. At the moment, I think what I need most is a way to make my work visible; I also need spiritual strength and the support of a system I can engage with and respect. The greatest challenge is accepting fate (laughs).

BAO: Finally, have you ever held any expectation or anticipation for what your artistic creations might offer this era in which we live?

YIN: I don't have any clear expectations. If art allows the soul to express itself, I only hope to continue creating. When I consider what I want to leave behind, I hope it's works that will enable us to participate in this era and inspire life and living.

4   ART

In the late 1990s, a fateful encounter with the renowned art historian Lü Peng marked a pivotal moment in Yin Jiulong's career. Through Lü Peng's monumental work *A History of 20th-Century Chinese Contemporary Art*, Jiulong began to grasp the evolving landscape of contemporary Chinese art and developed an ever-deepening interest in its expressive potential. This moment was an awakening, revealing to him the boundless possibilities of creative expression beyond the structured demands of design, where goals are often defined by clients. He was captivated by the freedom art offered—a liberation from external constraints, where expression could flow unfiltered and authentically from within.

This encounter ignited his desire to explore art as a path toward spiritual freedom, an impulse driven by the need to break from conventional creative boundaries. His art is guided by an inner compass, aiming to transcend the tangible and delve into realms of intuitive and transcendent expression. For Yin Jiulong, art is not merely a medium; it is the ultimate, ethereal language of the soul.

B·SIDE

THE
WORLD

I OFTEN GET BEATEN UP A
SOMETIMES I WANT TO H

PIP

《为自己立像
—经典主义0》

Mom's and Mine, 2023

190

Left *Fortune Cat, 2023*   *Adorable Cat, 2023*

Good Friends: Boy & Girl, 2023

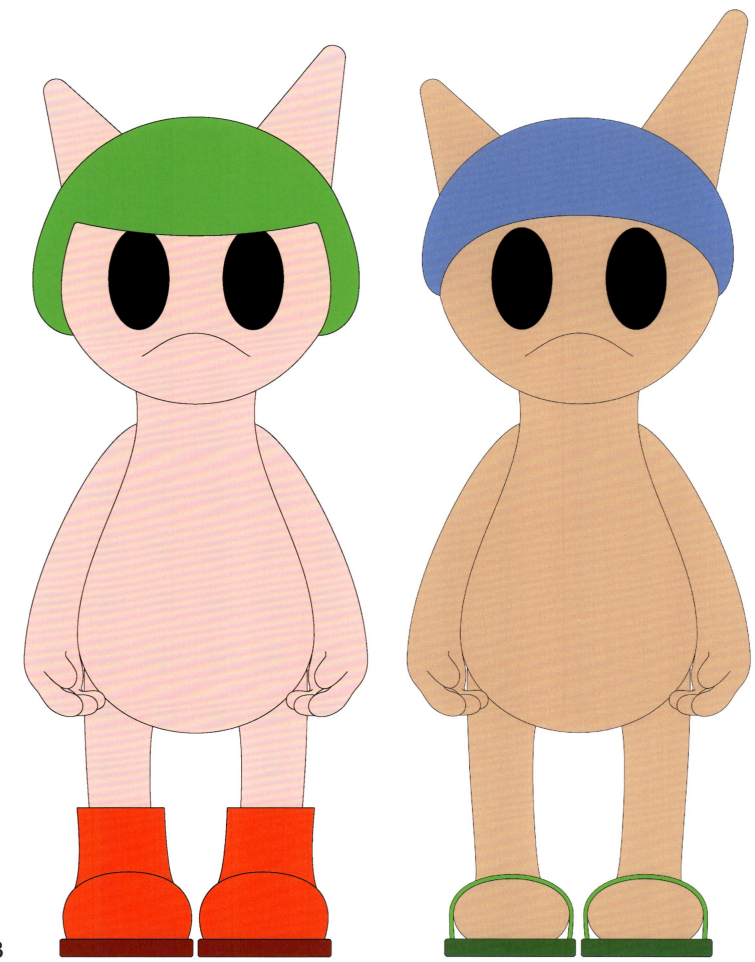

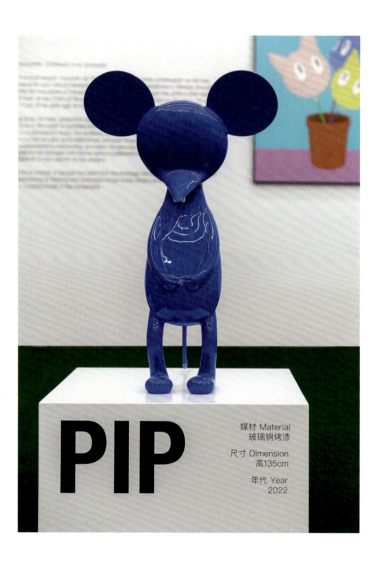

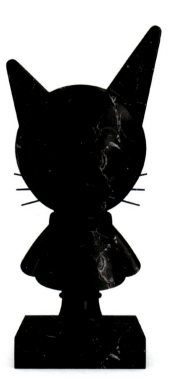

Sculpture for Self, 2023

Pip, 2022

Sculpture for Self, 2023

Next page *We're Different*, 2023

B.SIDE drawings and drafts

Sculpture production process, drawings,
and illustration drafts

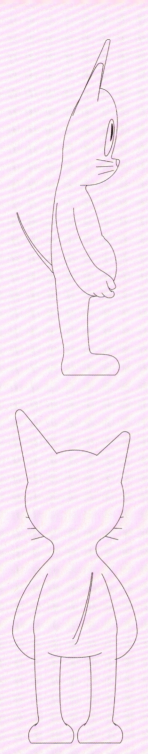

B.SIDE

For most people, childhood plays an integral role in shaping one's beliefs, values, and perceptions of the world. Characterized by material scarcity and a lack of culture, Yin Jiulong's childhood profoundly influenced his work. He describes the innocence of his youth stemming from a dialogue with nature, a baseline happiness infused with all too frequent moments of helplessness and pain. Despite many fond childhood memories, his early years also left him with numerous unutterable traumas. As a result, his recollections sometimes lead him to the conclusion that life's suffering outweighs its pleasures. While this perspective is perhaps not unique to Yin Jiulong, it is an interesting factor that motivated his natural willingness to do good in the world. His identity evolved through his ability to navigate and even draw inspiration from moments of transformation and confusion in the materially abundant, culturally diverse, and occasionally even fantastical world around us.

Trends come and go like the tides. Yin Jiulong has fashioned a new self-image: *B.SIDE*. Perhaps it is a way of making up for something missing in his childhood. Or perhaps, it is a means of revealing another side of himself to the world.

ONE FAMILY

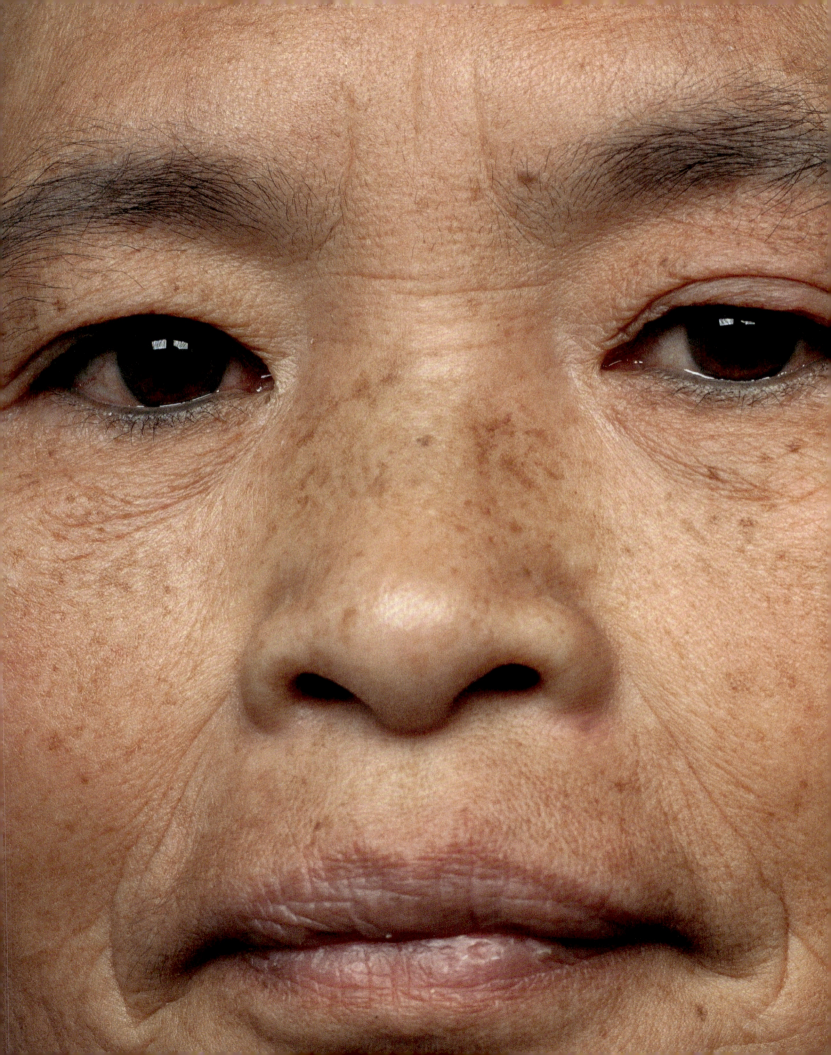

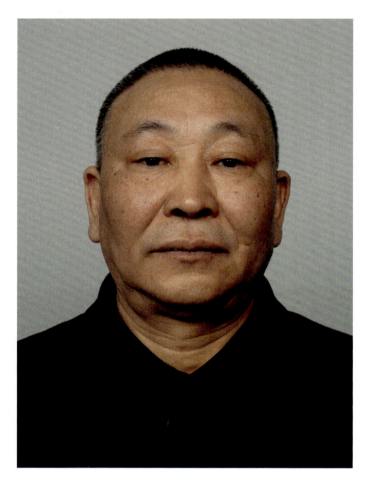

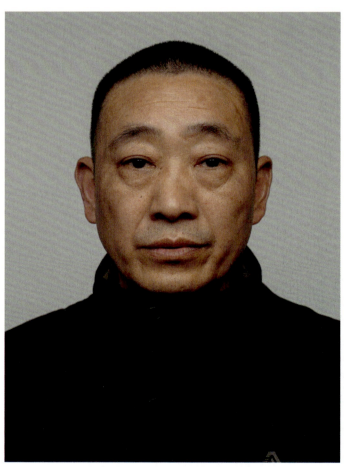

Big brother

Second big brother

Third big brother

Fourth big brother

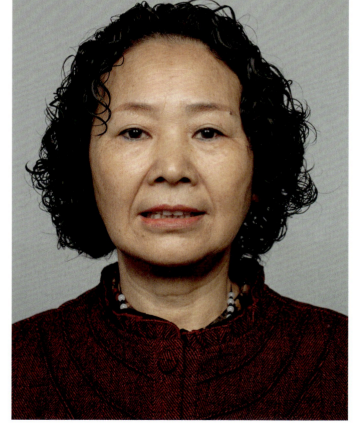

Yin Jiulong (the ninth child in his family)   Second big sister

Third big sister   Fourth big sister

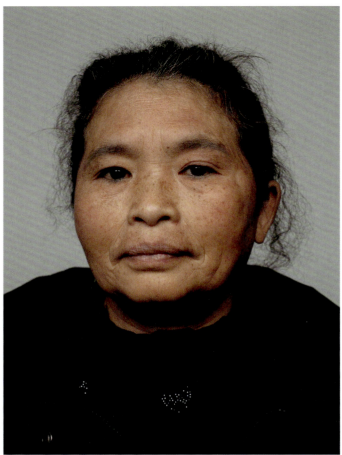

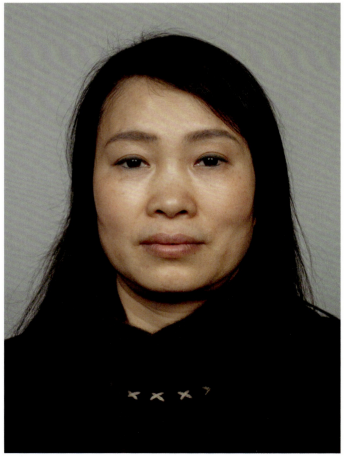

Big sister-in-law

Second big sister-in-law

Fourth big sister-in-law

Second big brother-in-law

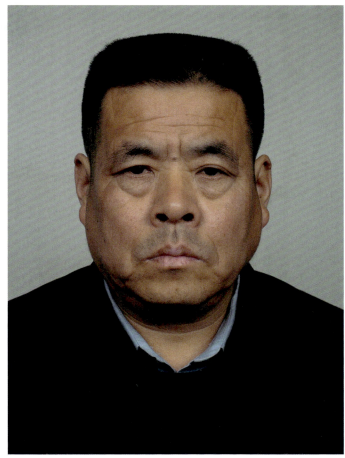

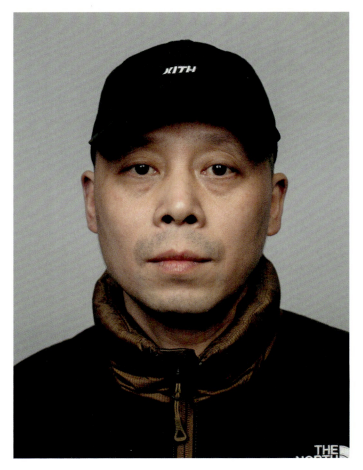

Third big brother-in-law

Son of big sister

Fourth big brother-in-law

Granddaughter of big sister

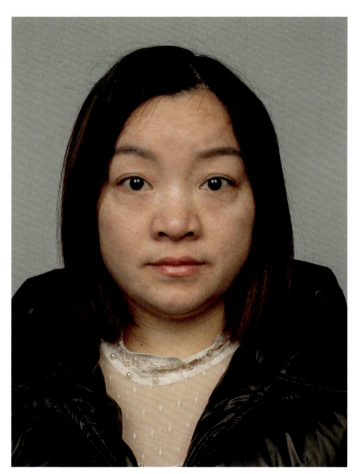

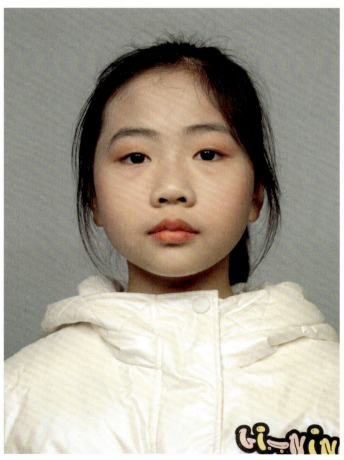

First son of second big sister

First daughter-in-law of second big sister

First granddaughter of second big sister

Second son of second big sister

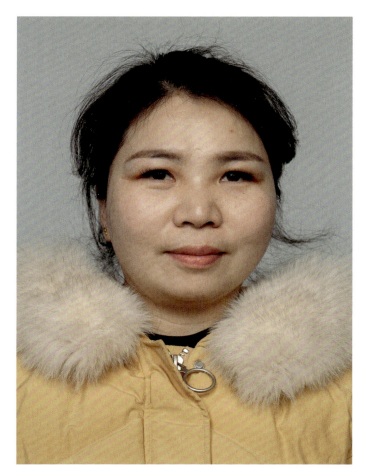

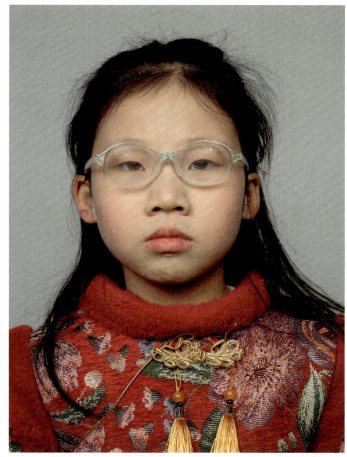

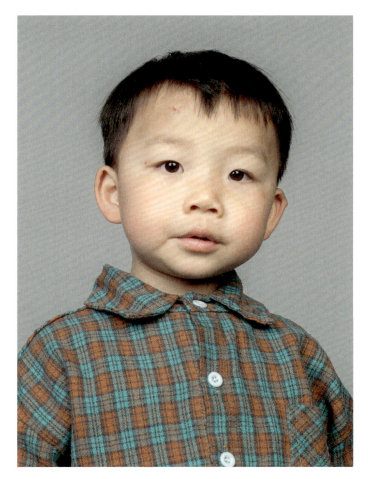

Second daughter-in-law of second big sister

Daughter of second son of big sister

Son of second son of big sister

Daughter of third big sister

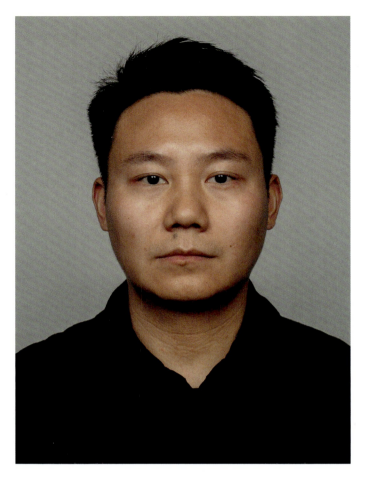

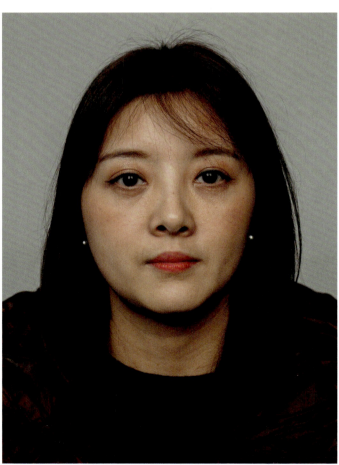

First son of fourth big sister

Second son of fourth big sister

Second daughter-in-law of fourth big sister

First daughter of second son of fourth big sister

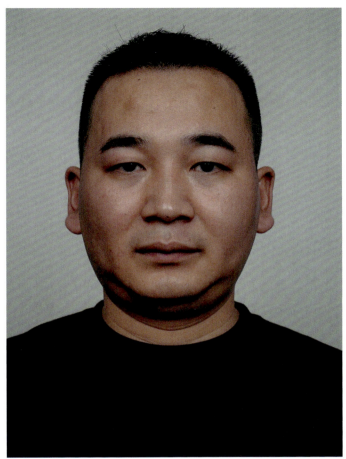

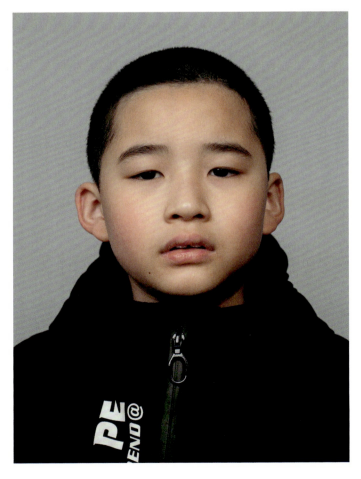

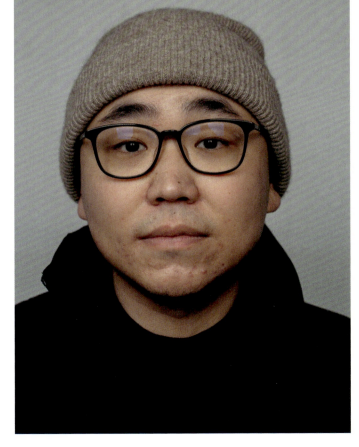

Second daughter of second son of fourth big sister

First son of big brother

Son of first son of big brother

Second son of big brother

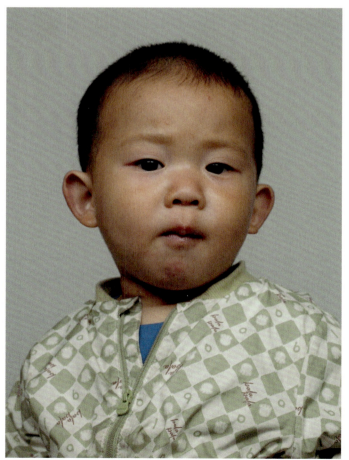

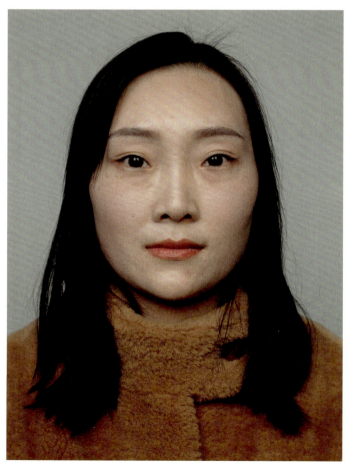

Son of second big brother

Daughter-in-law of second big brother

Grandson of second big brother

First daughter of third big brother

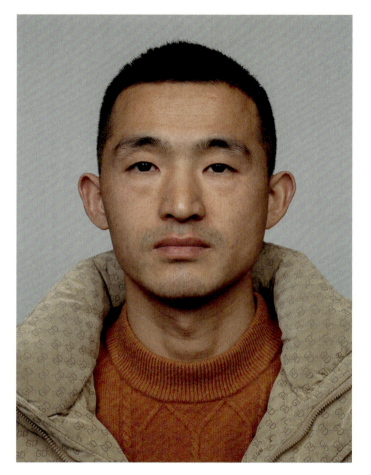

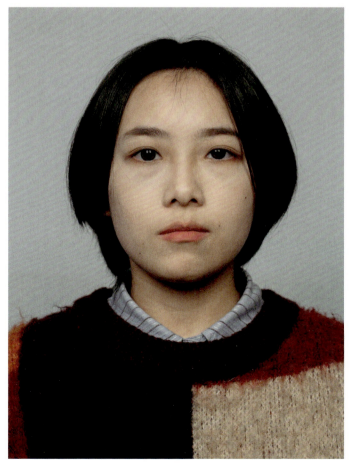

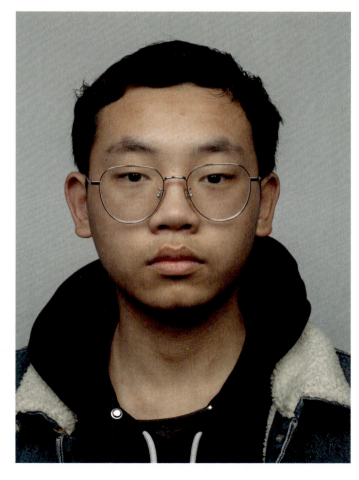

First son-in-law of third big brother

Daughter of first daughter of third big brother

Second daughter of third big brother

Third son of third big brother

Daughter of fourth big brother

Yin Jiulong's birthplace—a remote village in Sichuan, China.
The starting point of his *One Family* series

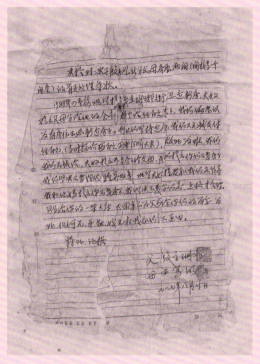

A document from their father confirming that
second brother is released from the obligation to
support his parents, following second brother's
decision to forgo his inheritance

Eldest sister (deceased)

Photo of the eldest sister (deceased) and
brother-in-law (deceased) on their wedding day

Mother and five sons

Four sisters

Yin Jiulong in his youth

Yin Jiulong in his rented apartment in Chengdu, 1997

Backstage

One Family is a record of three generations of Yin Jiulong's family: his own, and the generations that precede and follow him. It is an account of the illogical nature (or, perhaps, the self-contained logic) and allusive quality of the extended family, which is revealed to be a kind of switch, a path, an invisible but fundamental link connecting the psyches of modern people. Yin Jiulong was born in a large rural family of more than forty people with ages spanning seventy years. The family nucleus touched on politics, faith, identity, and the predicaments faced by individual members, often resulting in dispute and conflict. Far from giving rise to a new stable form, the difficulties brought by creeping urbanization into China's countryside, and the feelings of futility and envy in the face of these changes, seemingly replaced the modest stability of rural life with an unsettled state of rootlessness. As a result, the family form appeared both typical and peculiar, like an island in the middle of a volatile world. It had a complex relationship to the times, which raced forward while it lingered in the past. Yin Jiulong's return to the family in this work goes beyond the critical gaze of the rebel or runaway. Rather, it reveals an emotional turbulence only a deeper and more thorough exploration can uncover. Here, the artist observes one's being, the self and how they intertwine.

Yin Jiulong playing a minor role in a film production as a character in traditional costume, 1996

237

EVERYTHING IS OBTAINABLE

Props cast in resin

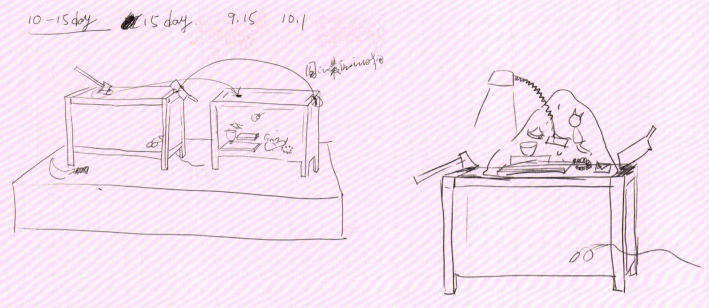

Everything Is Obtainable, design draft

Yin Jiulong with his mother, 2004

Everything Is Obtainable consists of two cabinets, one made of wood and another of transparent resin. The former is a relic of the artist's childhood in 1980s rural China, when every family had an old lockable cabinet in which they stored their valuable items: the limited oil, salt, rice, flour, and nuts they had been able to procure. What today appear to us as the most ordinary of products, were, at the time, the hard-earned resources a family needed to survive. An axe and a cleaver protrude from the wooden cabinet, as they used to appear when the artist was a child. They are not merely essential productive tools, but also potential weapons reflecting times of destitution when one's rights had to be fought for.

Cast from resin, the transparent cabinet displays a floating array of pieces and products: playthings from different eras, an imitation antique ceramic plate, an anal plug, a chain of silver beads, a photograph of the artist with his mother, a copy of the book *Yin Jiulong's Design*, a *B.SIDE* toy, a *gaiwan* teacup, and striped crockery. One's gaze is drawn toward the dramatic visual tension formed by this panoply of objects suspended in time.

Our lives are constantly being reconfigured based on what came before. Yin Jiulong has preserved this facet of modern life in the form of a time capsule containing individual cherished memories and the aspects of identity that can be articulated. The limited number of objects on display leads one to consider the possibility of a person also being succinctly summarized in this manner. *Everything Is Obtainable* is a metaphor for the obtainment of rights, the construction of a spiritual and material basis for life; a scene of our fates, dotted with glimmers of savagery, revealed by a consideration of who we are and the times in which we live.

THE PLAN OF EVERYTHING

No. 2, 2004 (detail)

BIOGRAPHY

Yin Jiulong has contributed to the global design sphere for over twenty-eight years. Since 1996, he has participated in numerous domestic and international art and design exhibitions and exchange activities, while also producing graphic design projects for a variety of international art and cultural organizations. At the same time, he has played a key role in the design and promotion of nearly all major art and cultural events in Chengdu. With projects spanning diverse creative fields, such as art, literature, products, and spaces, Jiulong strives to integrate art, design, and varied perspectives on life through his work.

2023   *B.SIDE Childhood*, *Portrait of Spring*, *Super Burn - Tianfu Contemporary Art Exhibition*, Tianfu Art Park, Chengdu, China
Everything Is Obtainable, *Kaleidoscope of Chinese Art*, Museo Irpino, Avellino, Italy
B.SIDE SEE YOU, Paint Your Shape: Invitational Exhibition, Chengdu Times Art Museum, Chengdu, China

2019   Ceramic work *m²*, Florence International Design Biennale (Chinese Edition), Ningbo Art Museum, Ningbo, China
DESIGN Is One: Artworks by Sun Chu and Yin Jiulong, Chongqing Yuan Art Museum, Chongqing, China
1/1000 series ceramics, Suzhou Creative Expo, Suzhou, China
Shambhala Cat Regional IP Design Project won the *Design Empowerment Person of the Year Award* (2019), awarded by Tsinghua University's New Culture Space
Awarded *"Innovative Fashion Creator of the Year"* by Chengdu Fashion Ceremony

2018   *ALL* (ceramic), *Design Shanghai*, Shanghai, China
Participated in the filming of *The New Imperial Palace* (Episode 6), which was broadcast
Interviewed for the documentary film *Craftsmanship*, broadcast on the CCTV network channel
Participated in the recording of *This Country's New Craftsman* (Episode 3), presented by Wu Xiaobo in association with Aqiyi, which was broadcast
Collaborated with the Chengdu Foreign Propaganda Department and Chengdu TV to film the personal promotional video *Chengdu Women in Yin Jiulong's Eyes*, broadcast on Phoenix America, Phoenix Europe, and Hong Kong ATV

| 2017 | *Hello Delft*, *Buddha is Gone*, and *Flow, Imperial Kilns - Exhibition for the Royal Family*, Prince Delft Memorial Museum, Delft, the Netherlands
Art residency work *Flow* is included in the collection of Queen Marieke Jaerma of the Netherlands
More Than New (Tea and Coffee Makers for Covered Bowls), Design Shanghai, Shanghai, China
Awarded *"The Most Popular Figure"* by *Today's Headlines* |
|---|---|
| 2016 | *1/1000* and *Song, The Road of Time - New Crafts/Creativity and Sustainable Development in China*, Qingcheng Mountain, Chengdu, China
Artisan Trio Exhibition - Ceramics by Yin Jiulong, Hengshan Heji, Shanghai, China
1/1000 and Song Ceramics Exhibition, Design Shanghai, Shanghai, China
Invited to participate in the Delft Blue Ceramic Art Residency Project at the Prince Delft Memorial Museum in the Netherlands |
| 2015 | *1/1000 and Song Ceramics Exhibition* and *A Portrait of Spring*, *Hangzhou International Design Week*, Hangzhou Yintai In77, Hangzhou, China
A Portrait of Spring, *The Tower in the Sky: Art + 3D Printing + Exhibition*, Chengdu Museum of Contemporary Art, Chengdu, China
1/1000, *FROM MING TO MODERNITY - When Tradition Meets Design*, China Design Centre, London, UK
1/1000 and *Dream-Sky*, *Phase - Diffractive Ecology Exhibition*, Taikoo Li Ocean Express, Chengdu, China
Awarded *"Chengdu's Fashionable Figure"* by *Bund Pictorial* - Chengdu Fashion |
| 2014 | *1/1000*, *Different Colors Exhibition*, Shanghai, China
Ink, *Paper Medium Invitational Exhibition*, Aihe Rawei Art and Life Museum, Chengdu, China
1/1000 Yin Jiulong Ceramics Exhibition, Ai & Ravi Art & Living Museum, Chengdu, China
1/1000, *High Ridge: Special Invitation Exhibition*, *Design Shanghai*, Shanghai, China |
| 2013 | *Dream - Sky*, *Endless, Art Scene - Yin Jiulong & Rongtao's Art Scene*, Five Oxes Visual and Packaging Institute, Chengdu, China
Designs by Yin Jiulong Ceramics Exhibition, Tiexiangsi Water Street, Chengdu, China |
| 2012 | Solo Exhibition of Yin Jiulong's Designs, Chengdu Museum of Contemporary Art, Chengdu, China
The series of ceramic works *1/1000* was collected by Chengdu Museum of Contemporary Art. In the same year, Yin Jiulong's personal design work collection was published. |
| 2010 | Three poster designs were selected for the *1st German-Chinese Biennale of Graphic Design 2010*, Offenbach, Germany |
| 2006 | *Sending* (installation), *Paper Creativity Exhibition*, Chengdu, China |

Translation:
Zhi Shen
Stephen Nashef

Copyediting and Proofreading:
Alexia Petsinis

Photo Credits:
Xiao Quan: p. 22
Guan Li: pp. 71, 73, 74, 87, 91, 99, 100, 105
Liang Cang: p. 80
Liu Wei: pp. 141, 146, 184, 196, 197, 198, 199, 202, 244–253
Chen Chunlin: pp. 206–219
Ma Zhandong and Chen Jie: pp. 222–235

Art Direction:
Al mare. Studio

Layout:
Chen Yiqiang

Editorial Coordination:
Manuela Schiavano

© 2025 Mondadori Libri S.p.A.
Distributed in English throughout the World by
Rizzoli International Publications, Inc.
49 West 27th Street
New York, NY 10001
www.rizzoliusa.com

ISBN: 978-88-918401-4-1

Printed in Italy
2025 2026 2027 2028 / 10 9 8 7 6 5 4 3 2 1

Visit us online:
Instagram.com/RizzoliBooks
Facebook.com/RizzoliNewYork
X: @Rizzoli_Books
Youtube.com/user/RizzoliNY

This book is dedicated to everyone who has been part of my journey, with special gratitude to my family.

It represents the culmination of nearly thirty years of work—a journey marked by reflections, moments of anxiety, and the uncertainties that accompany each stage of life. In many ways, it is the outcome of a restrained struggle for existence.

I extend my heartfelt thanks to Mr. Lü Peng, Bao Qian, Manuela Schiavano, and to all who, though not named here, contributed to my early work.

This book is also for those on their own journeys, striving to move forward.